THE ALPHABET LETTER TRACING BOOK

Trace the letters with a pencil

A

A 1 2 3

Trace the letters with a pencil

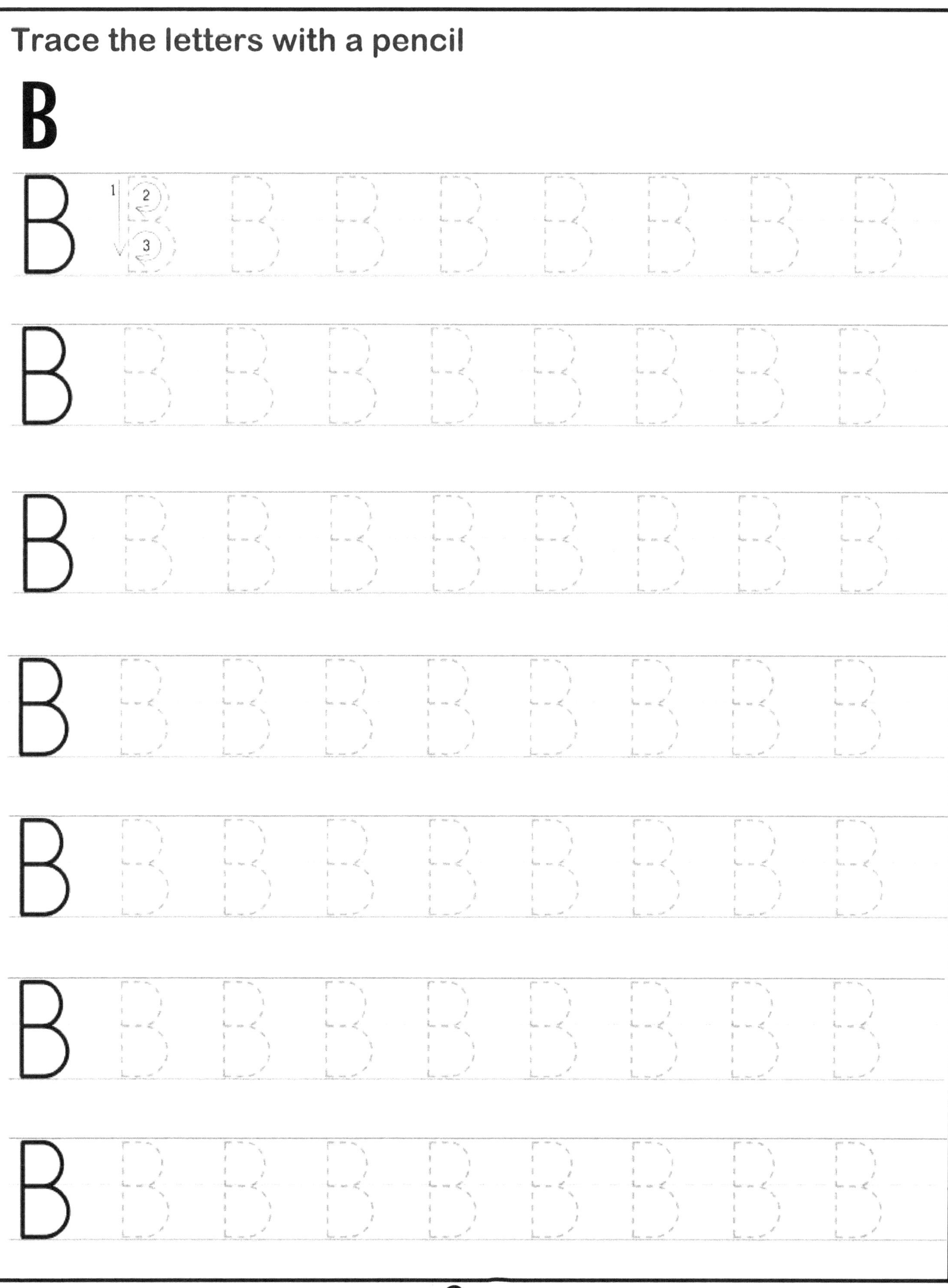

Trace the letters with a pencil

C

C C C C C C C C C
C C C C C C C C C
C C C C C C C C C
C C C C C C C C C
C C C C C C C C C
C C C C C C C C C
C C C C C C C C C

Trace the letters with a pencil

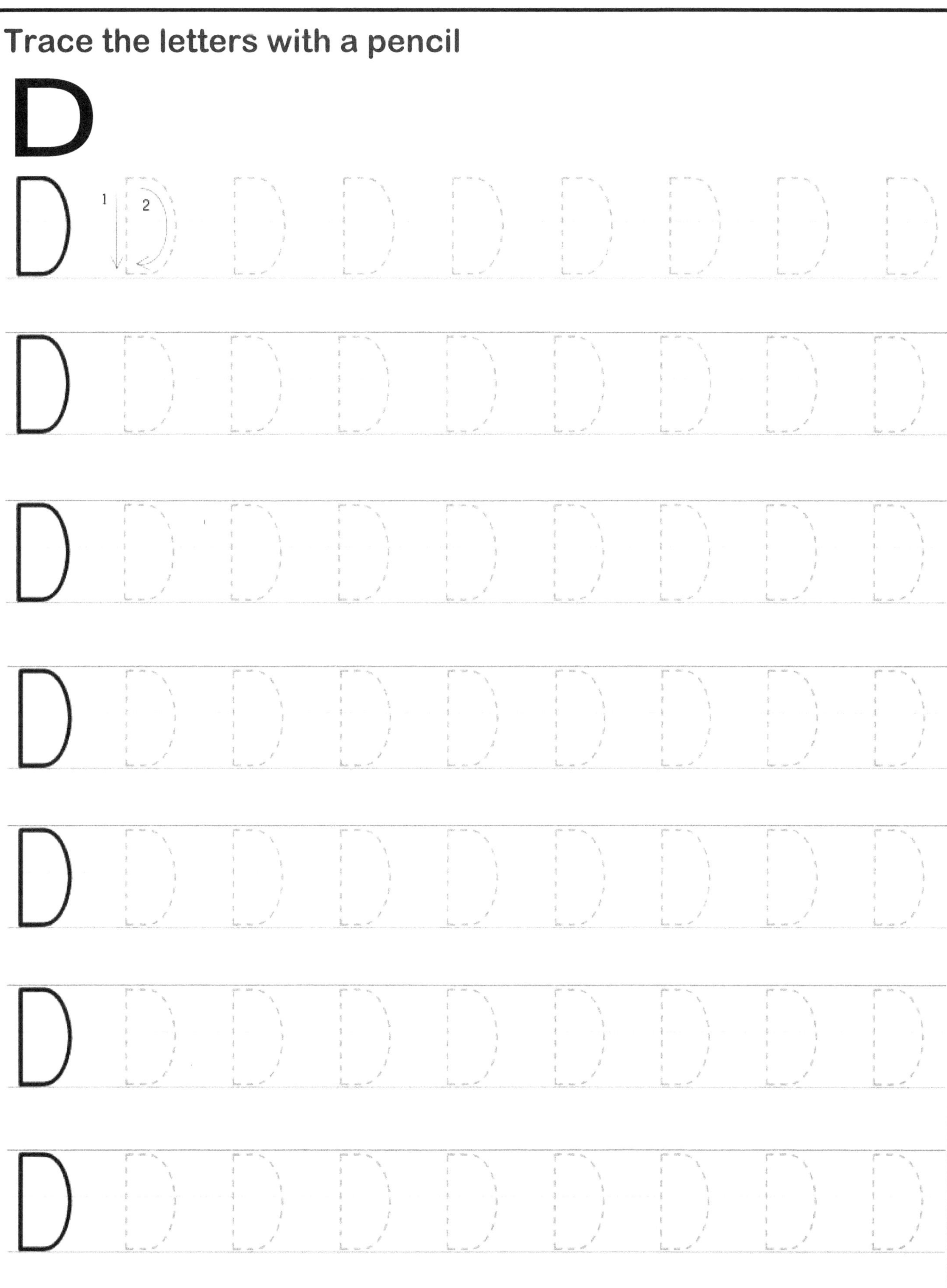

Trace the letters with a pencil

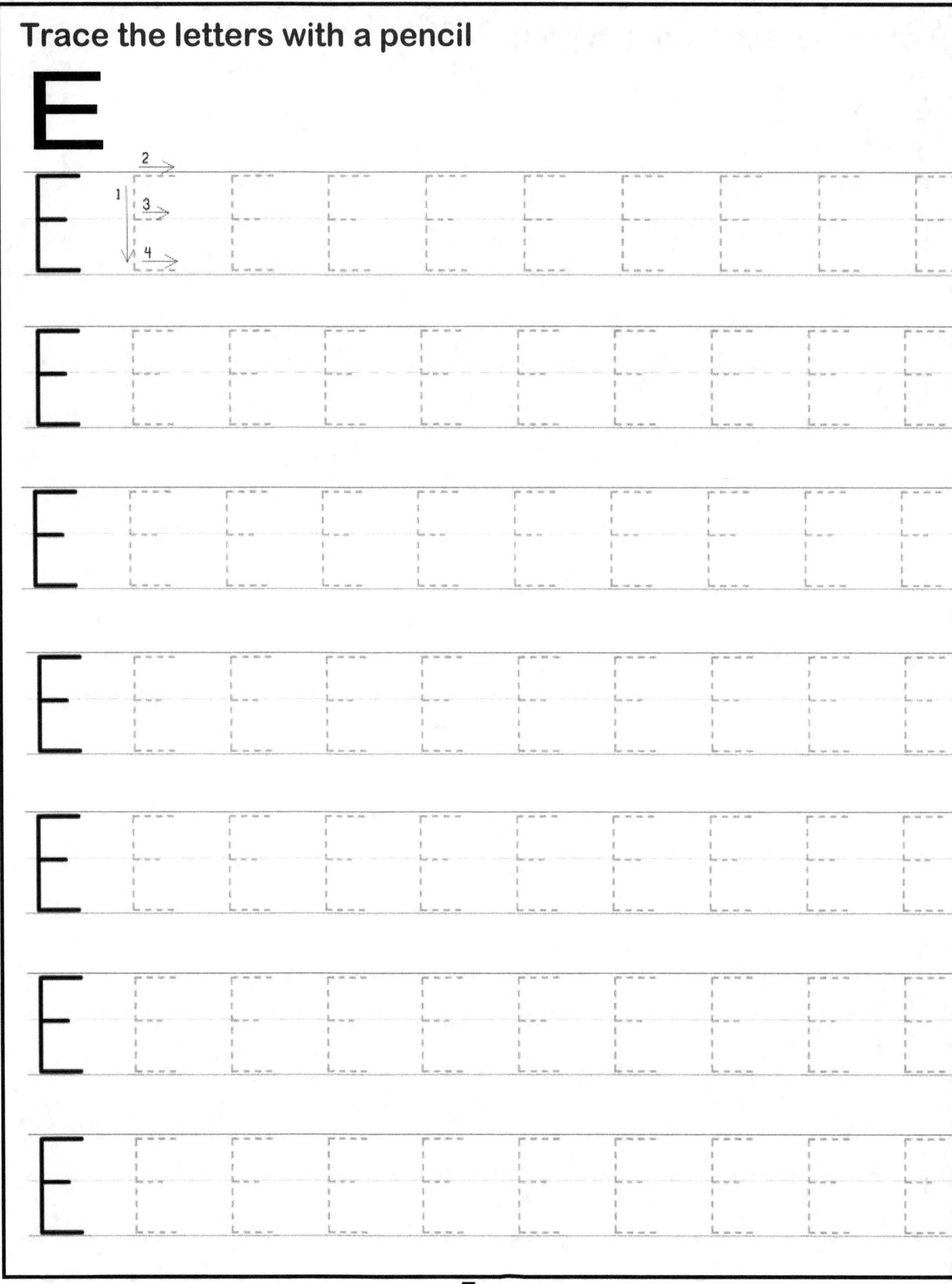

Trace the letters with a pencil

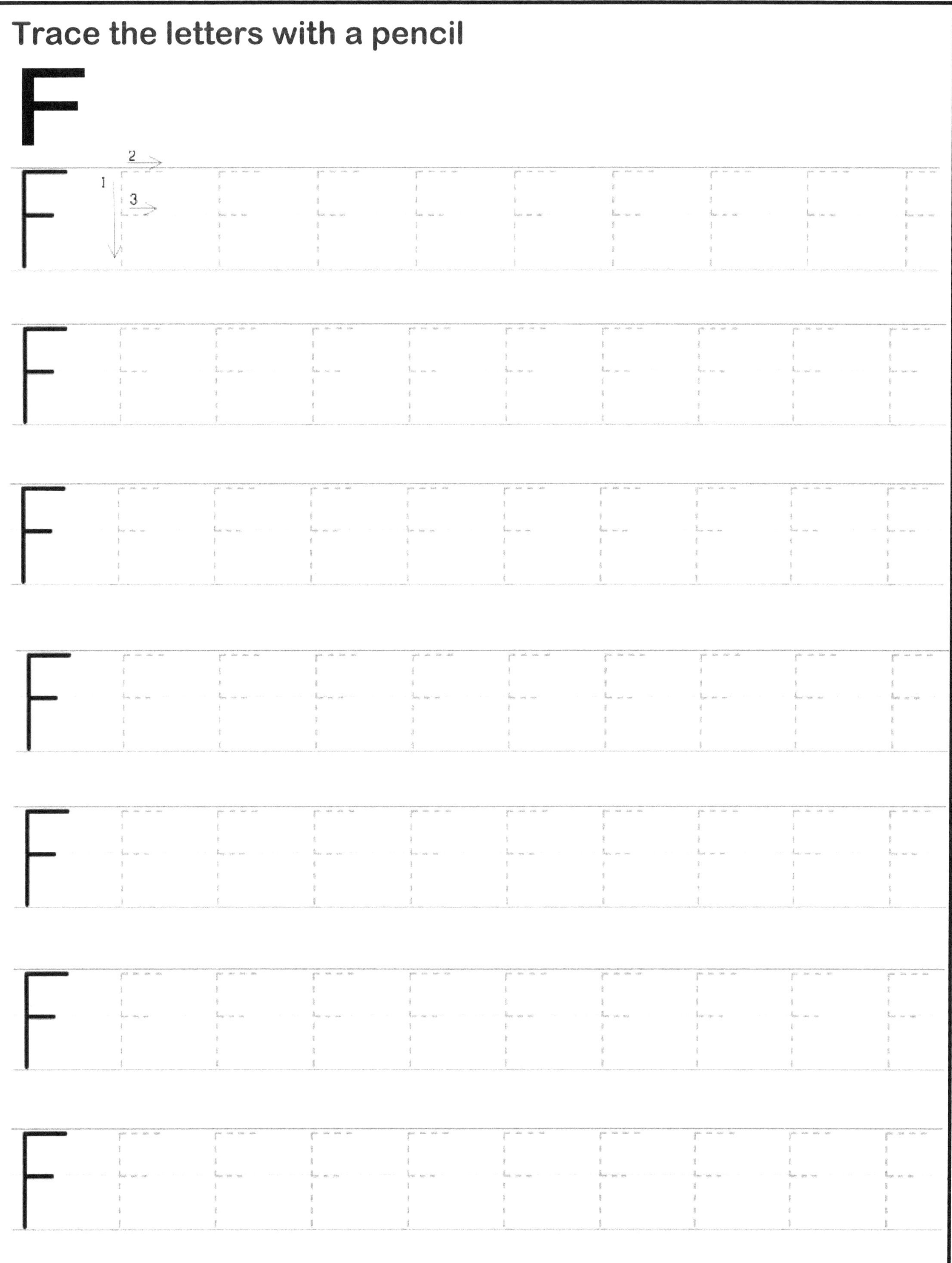

Trace the letters with a pencil

G

G
G
G
G
G
G
G

Trace the letters with a pencil

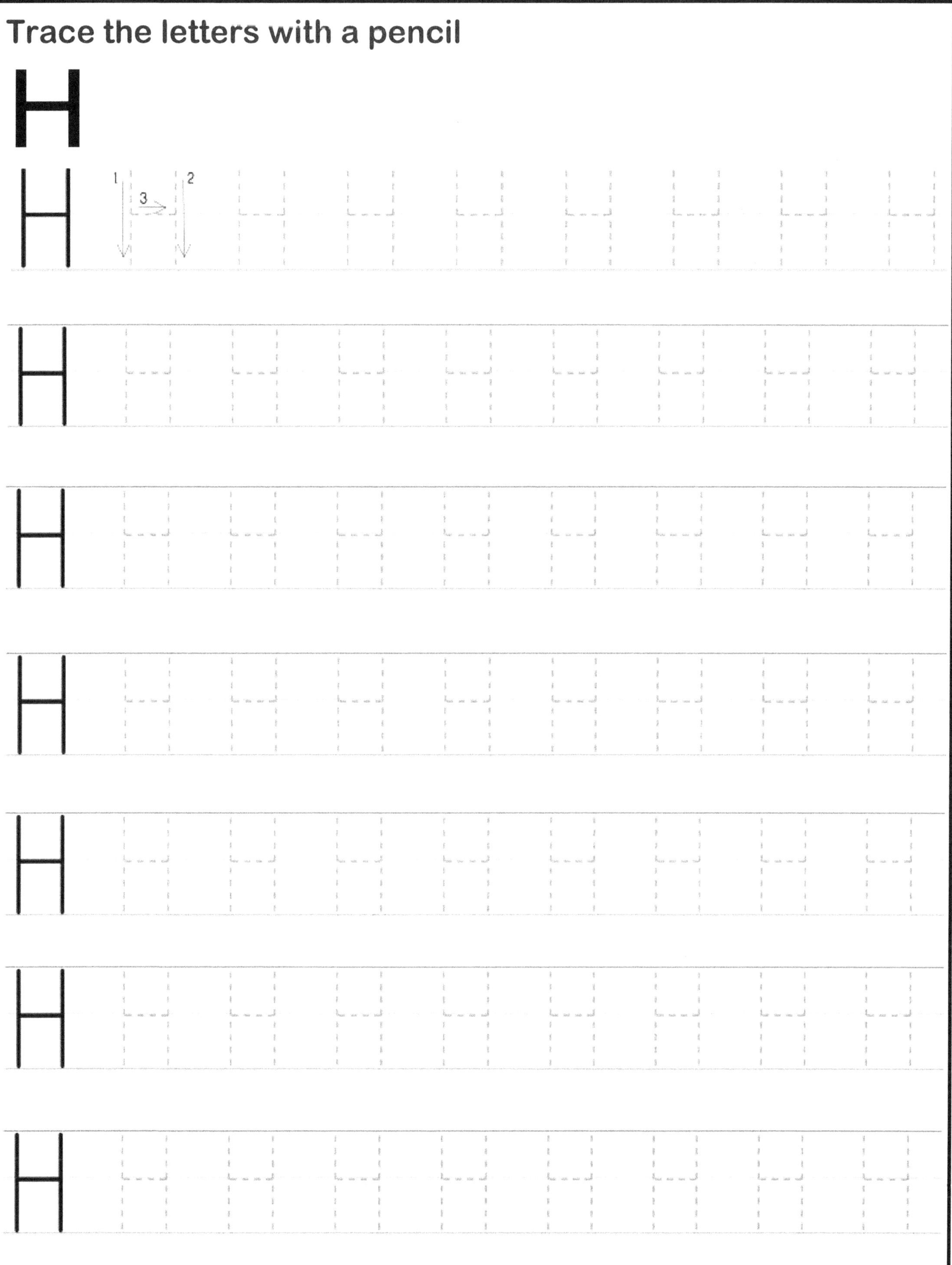

Trace the letters with a pencil

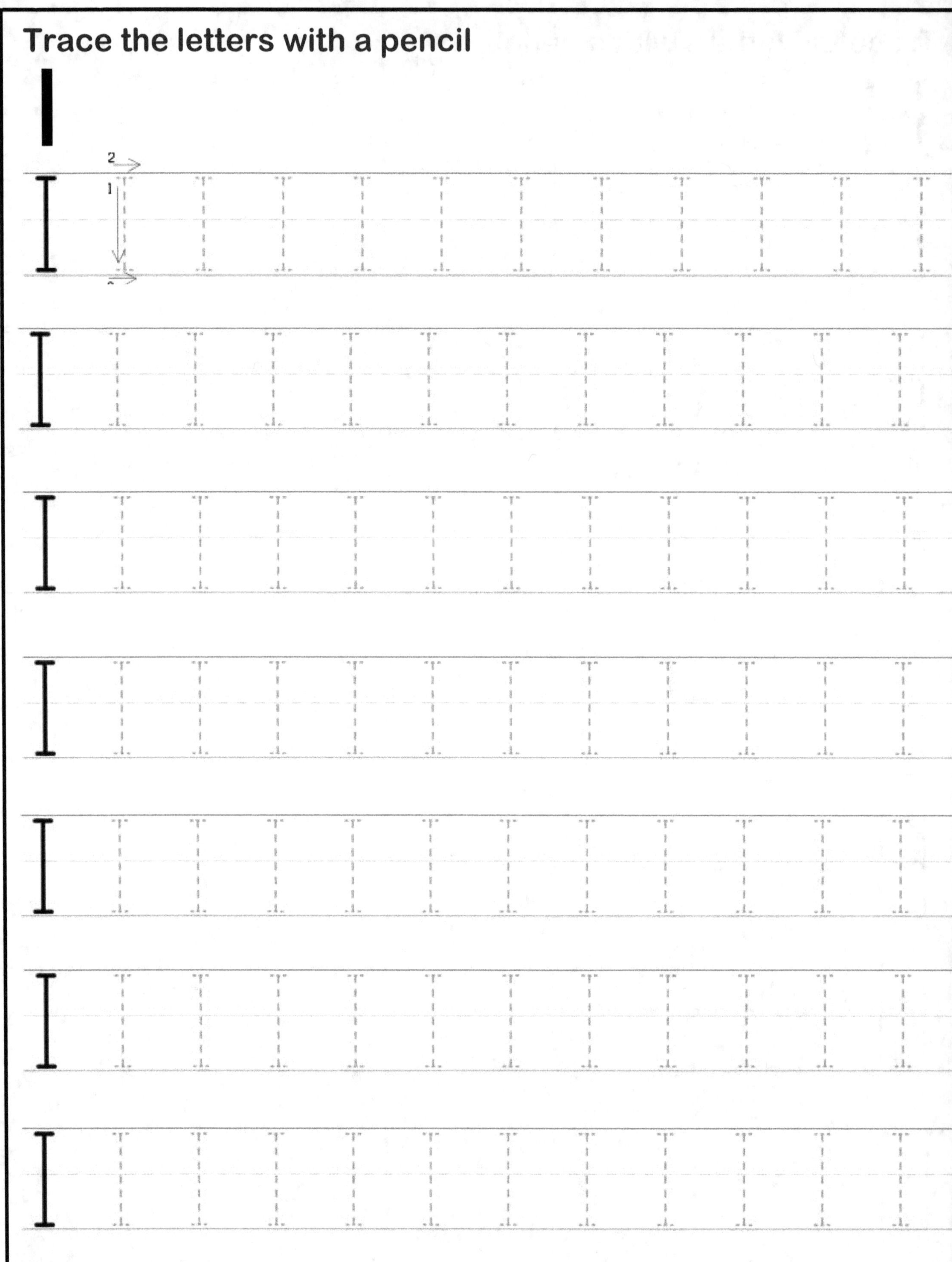

Trace the letters with a pencil

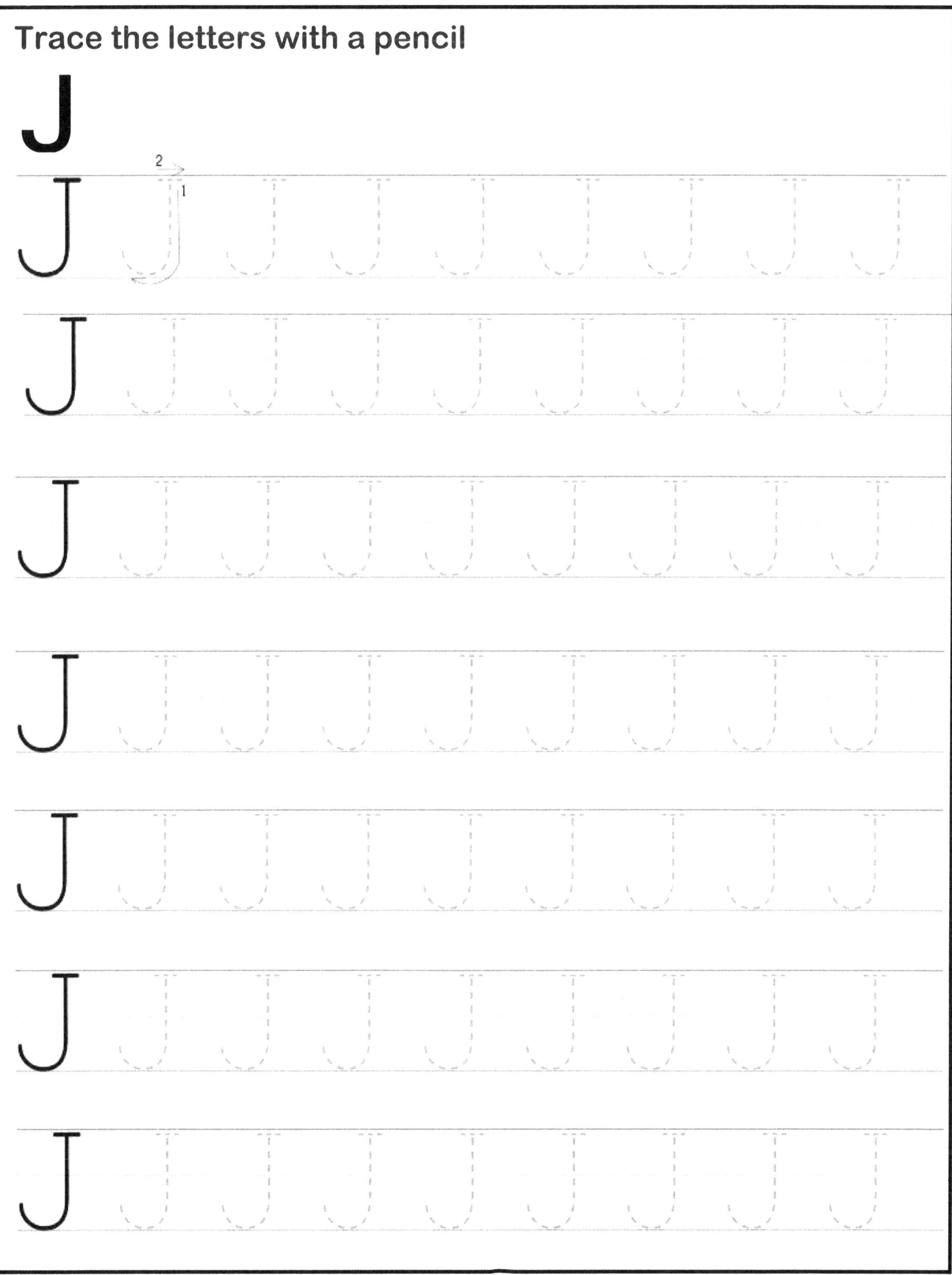

Trace the letters with a pencil

K

K 1 2 3

K

K

K

K

K

K

Trace the letters with a pencil

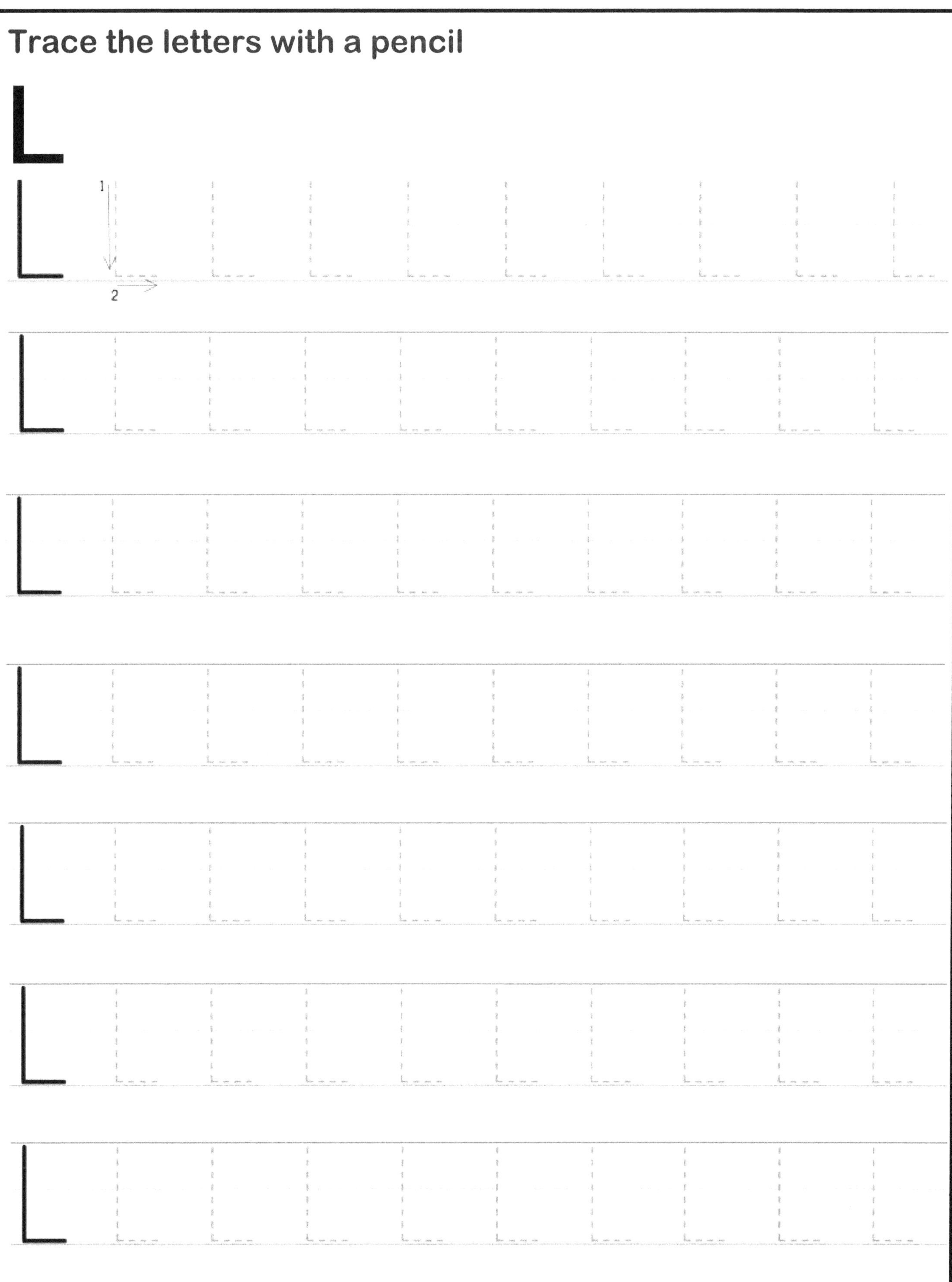

Trace the letters with a pencil

M

M 1 2 4 3

M

M

M

M

M

M

Trace the letters with a pencil

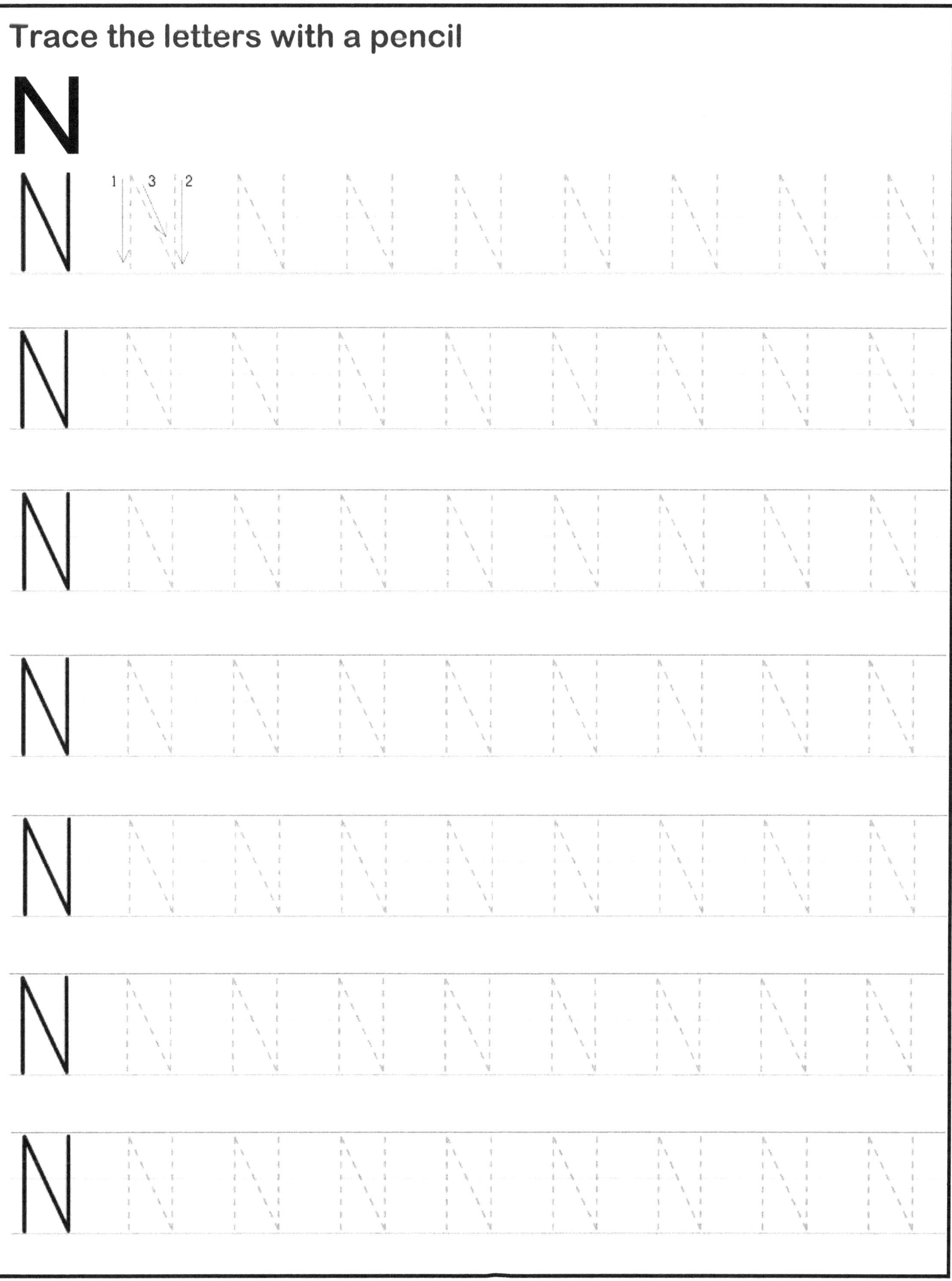

Trace the letters with a pencil

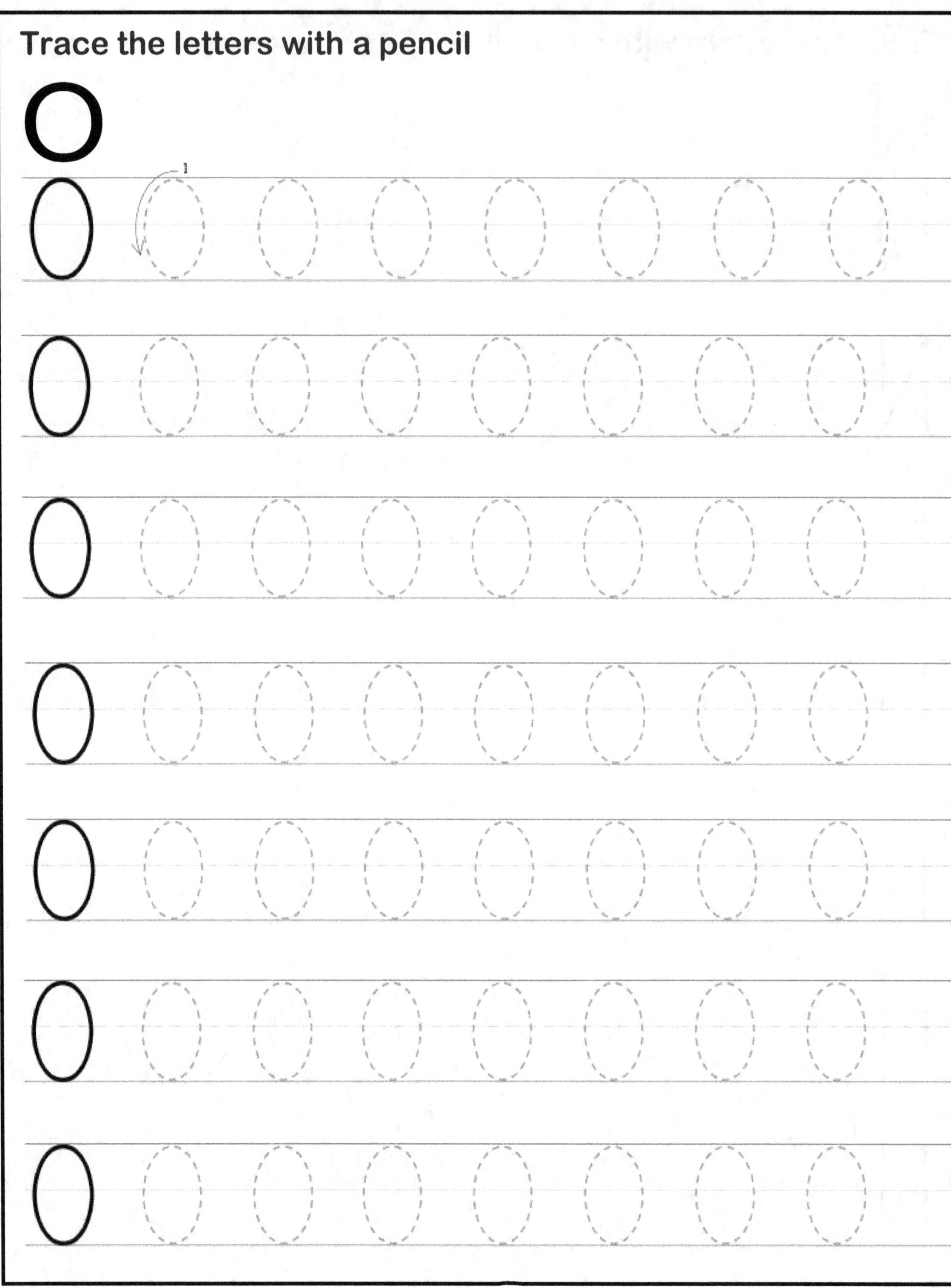

Trace the letters with a pencil

P

Trace the letters with a pencil

Q

Q

Q

Q

Q

Q

Q

Q

Trace the letters with a pencil

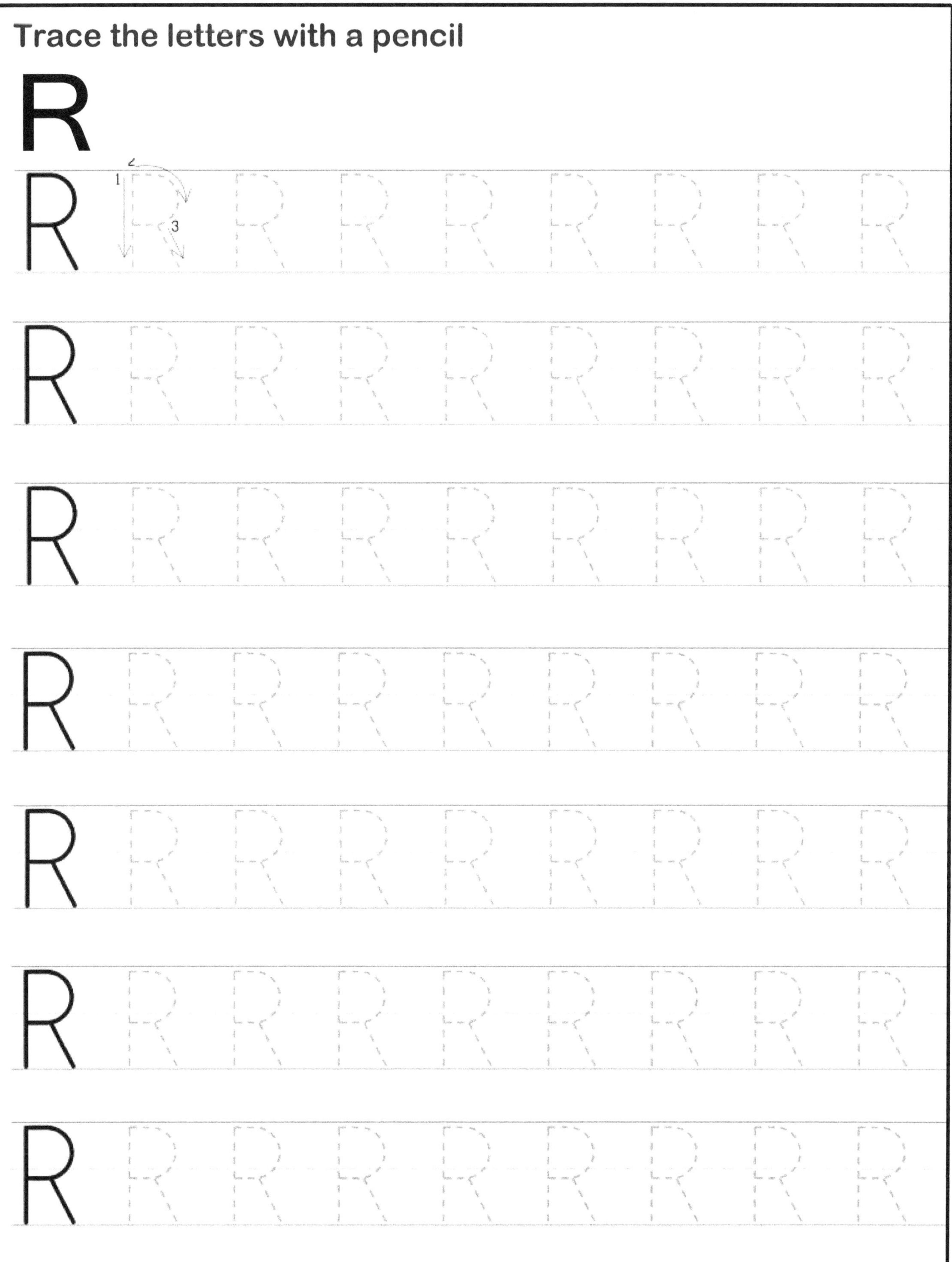

Trace the letters with a pencil

S

S

1

S

S

S

S

S

S

Trace the letters with a pencil

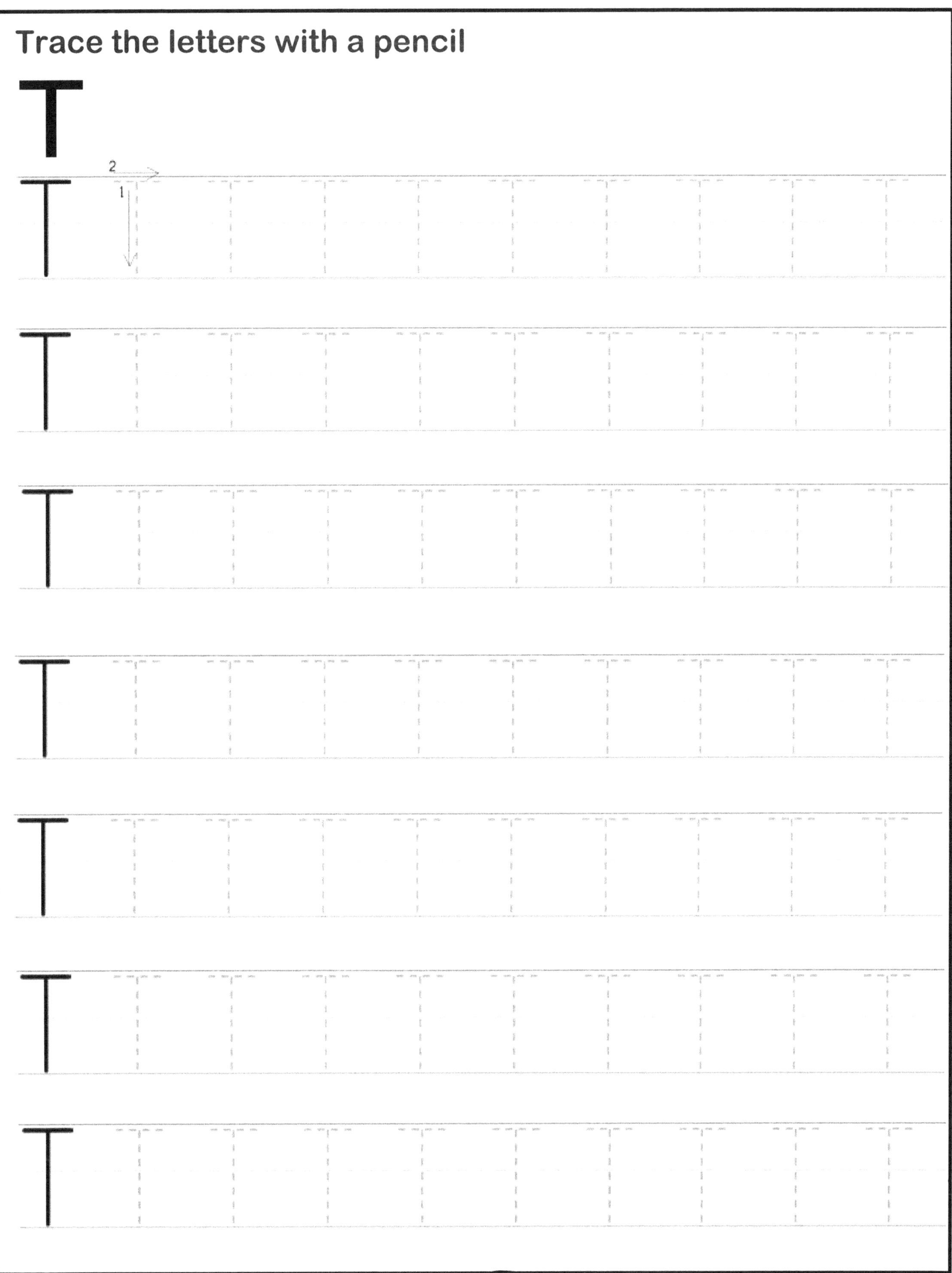

Trace the letters with a pencil

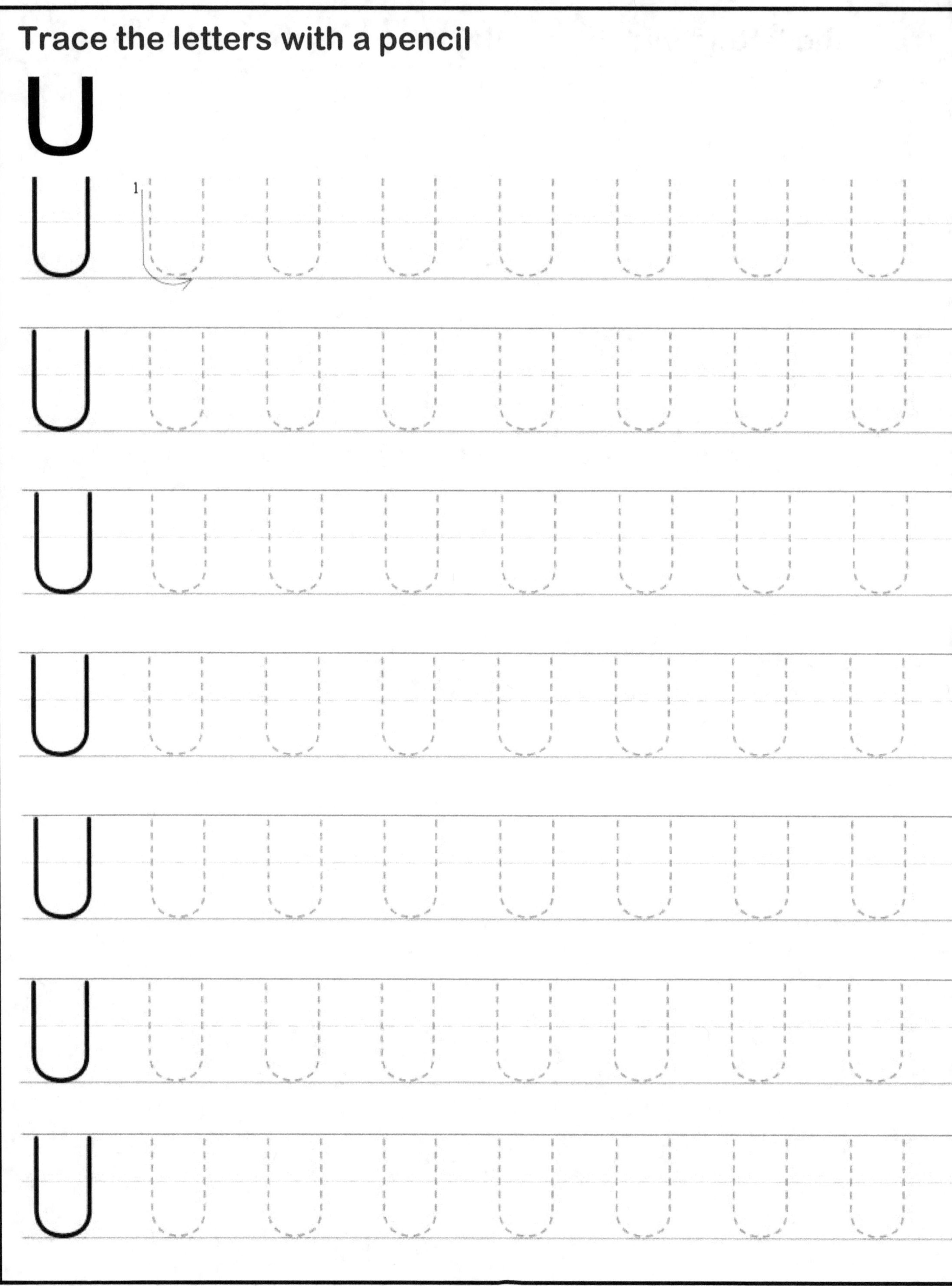

Trace the letters with a pencil

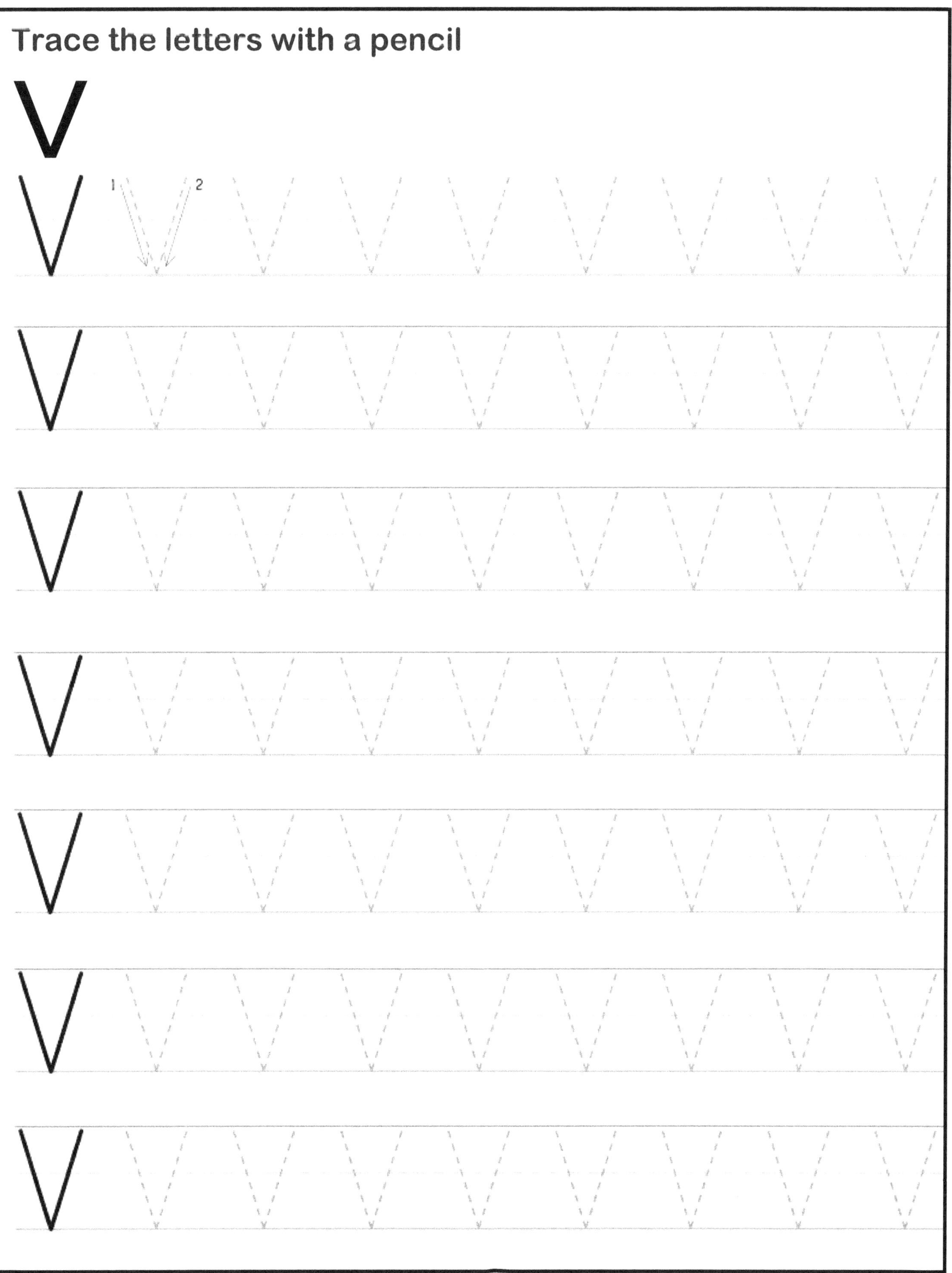

Trace the letters with a pencil

W

W 1 2 3 4

W

W

W

W

W

W

Trace the letters with a pencil

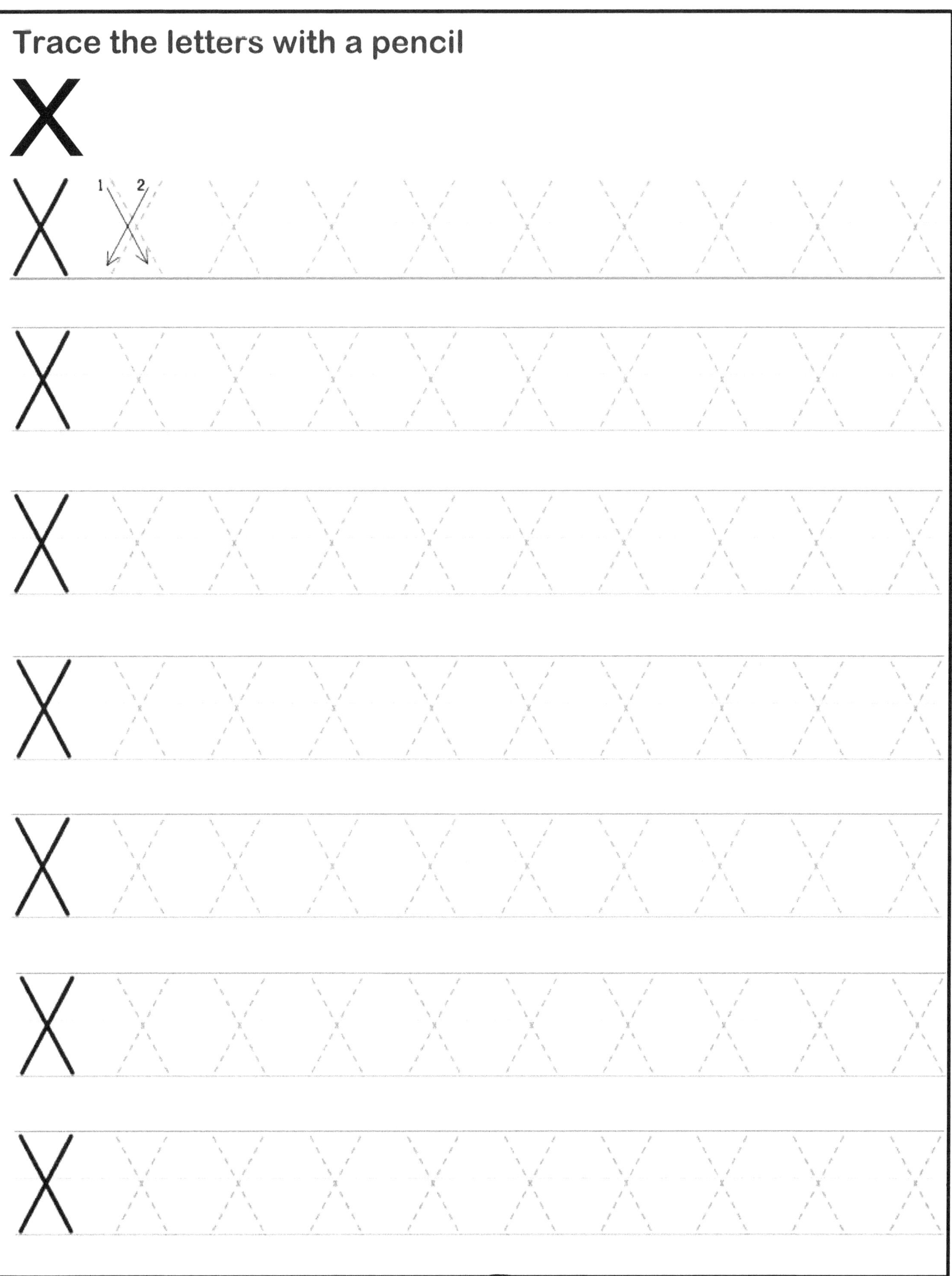

Trace the letters with a pencil

Y

Y 1 2 3

Y

Y

Y

Y

Y

Y

Trace the letters with a pencil

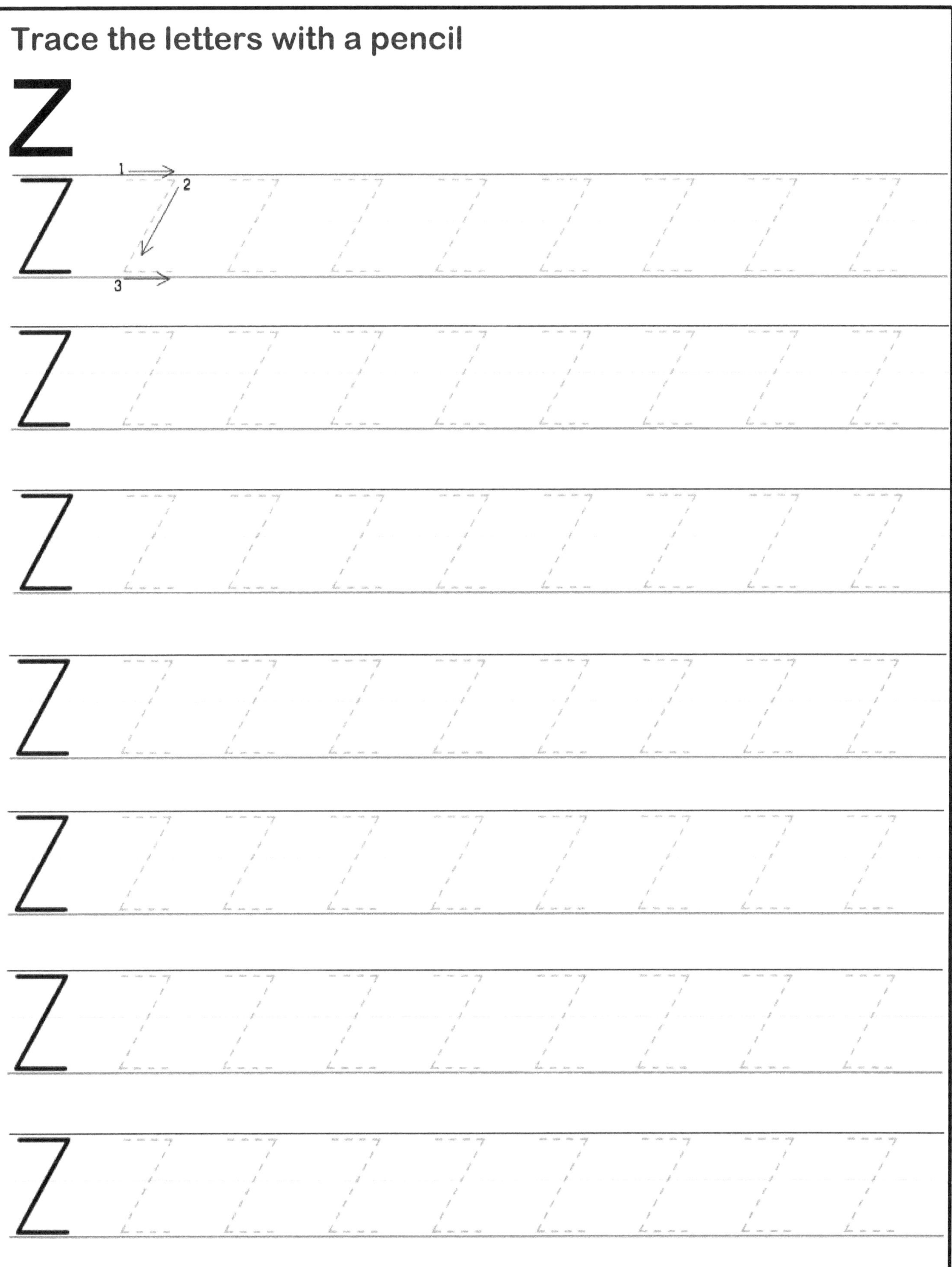

Trace the letters with a pencil

Trace the letters with a pencil

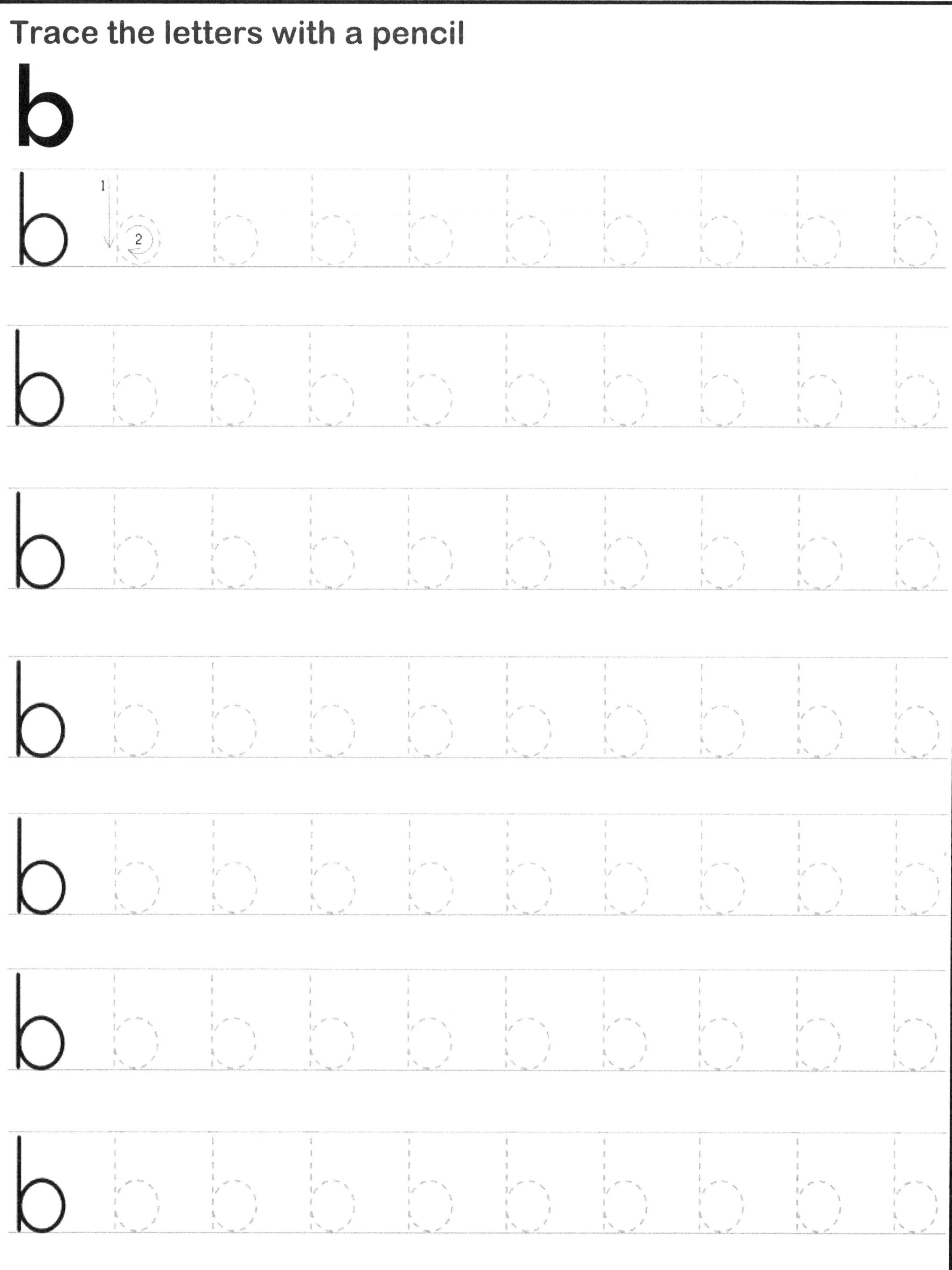

Trace the letters with a pencil

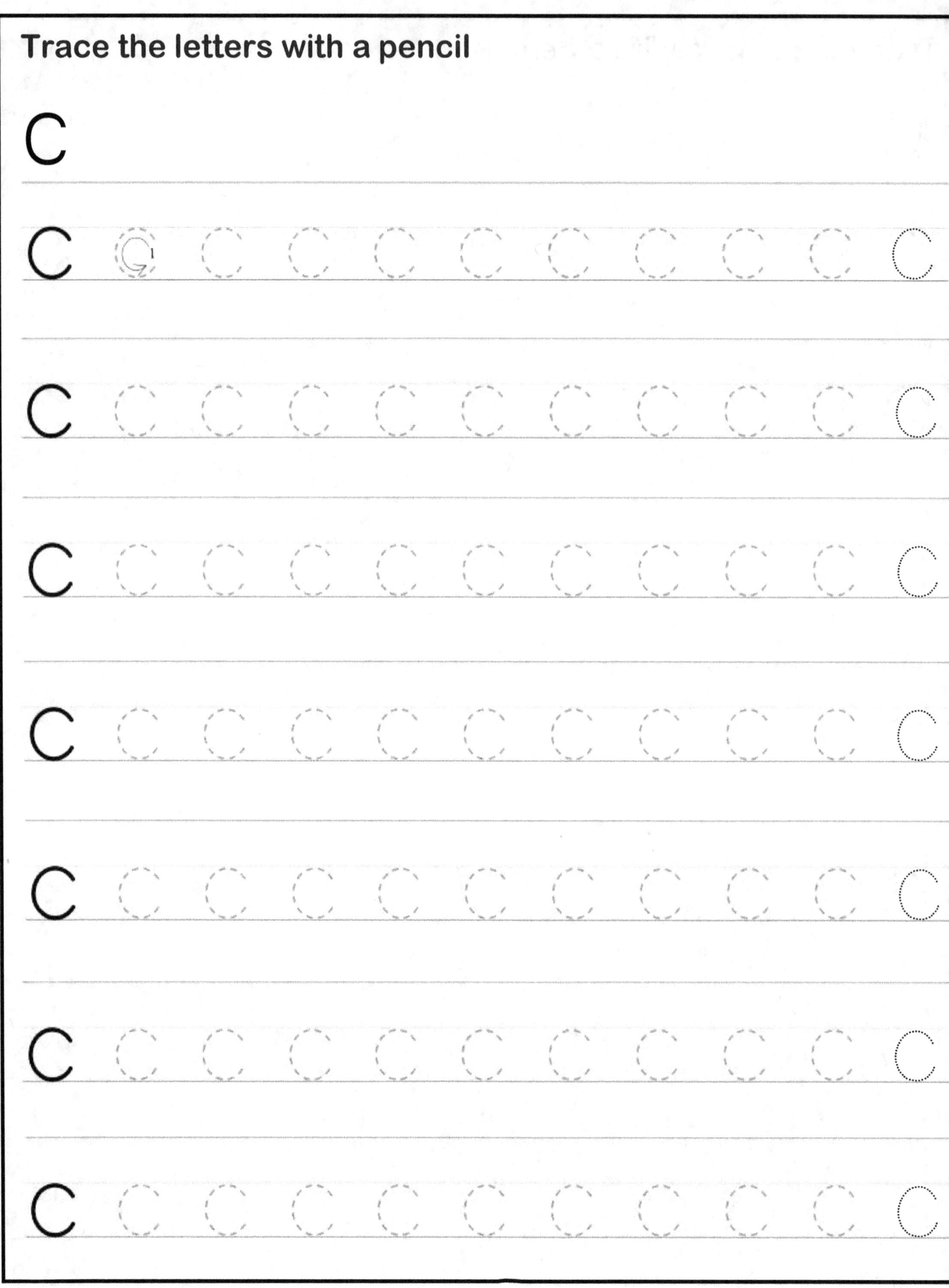

Trace the letters with a pencil

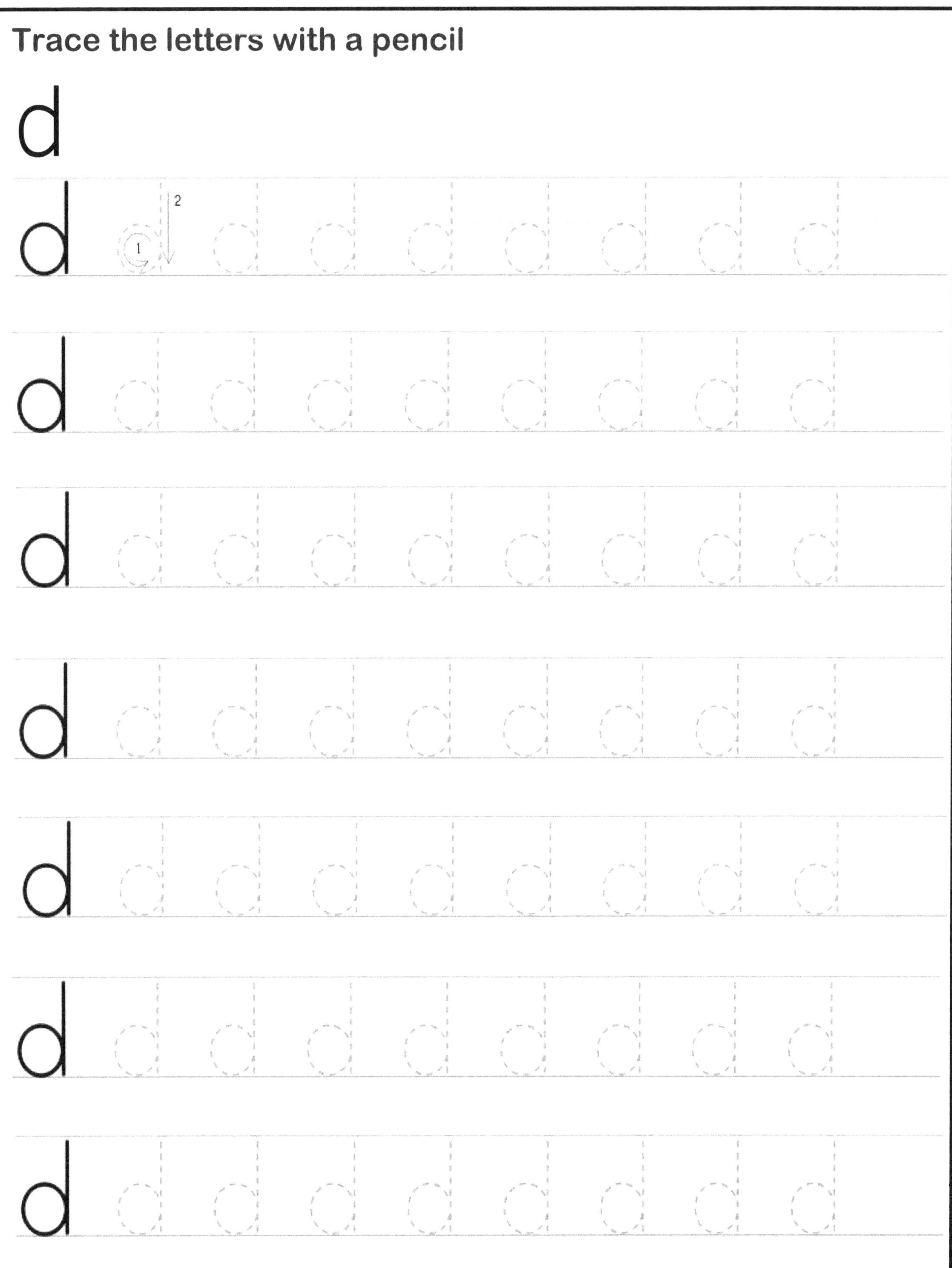

Trace the letters with a pencil

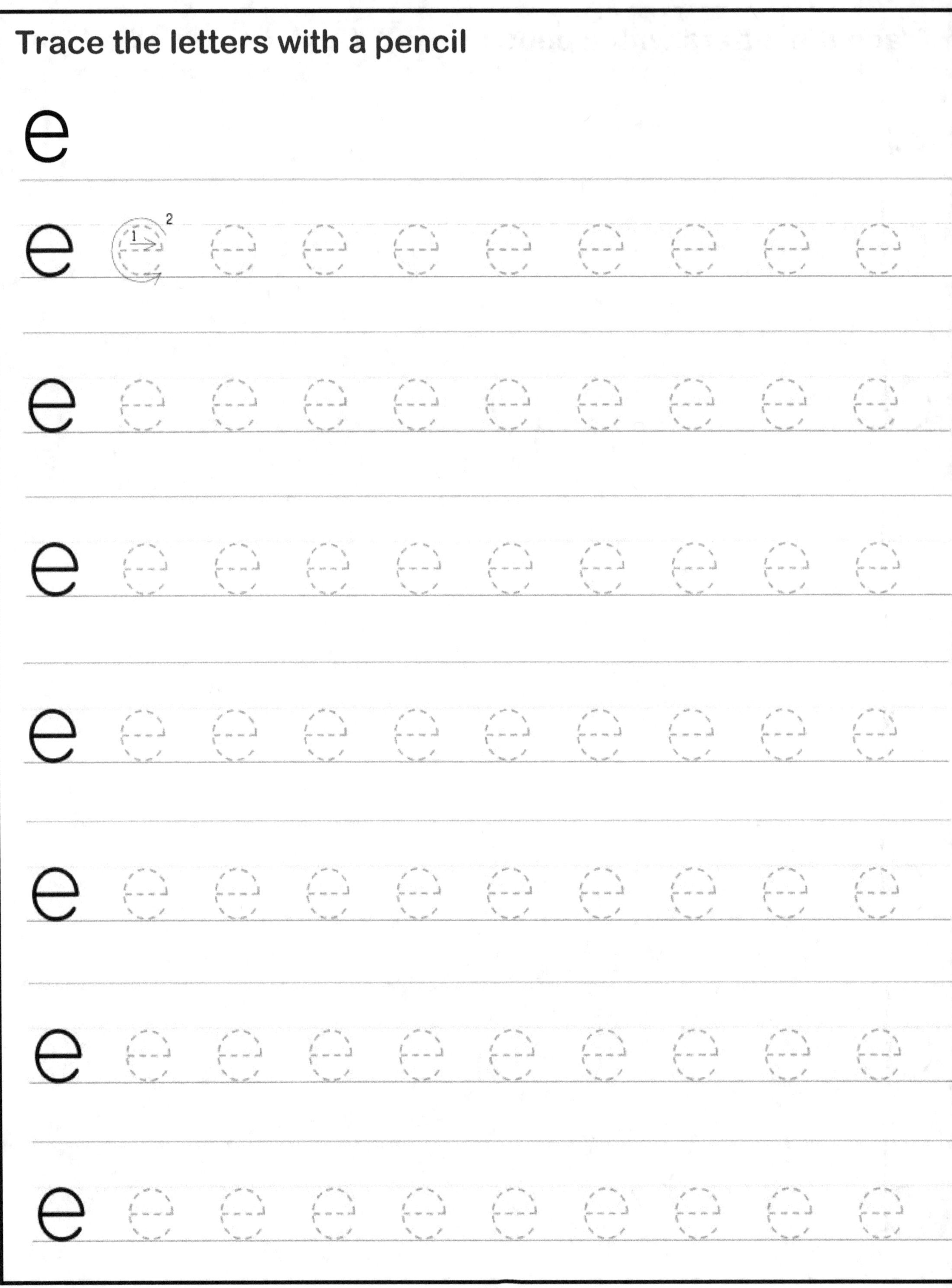

Trace the letters with a pencil

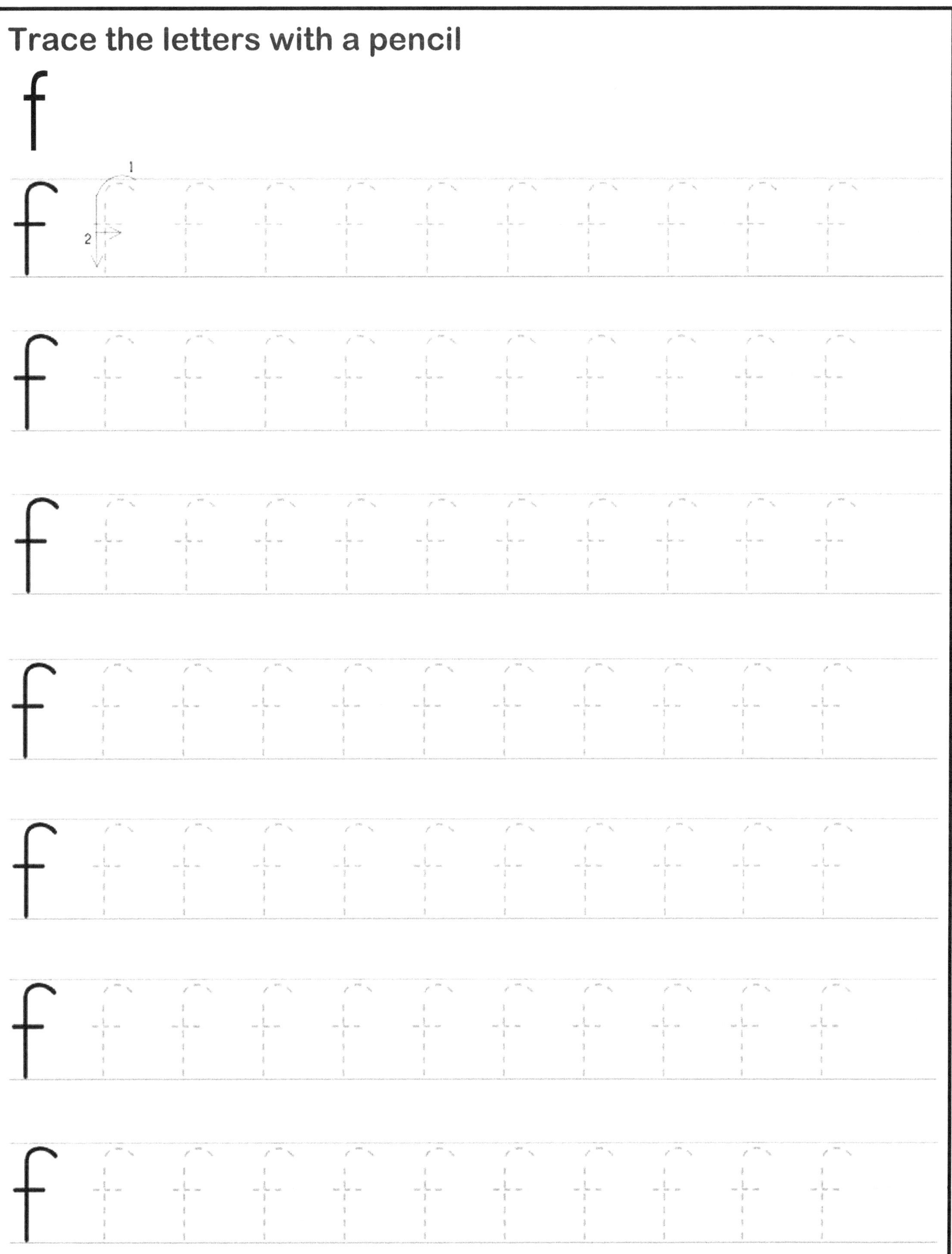

Trace the letters with a pencil

g

g 1 2

g

g

g

g

g

g

Trace the letters with a pencil

h

h 1 2

h

h

h

h

h

h

Trace the letters with a pencil

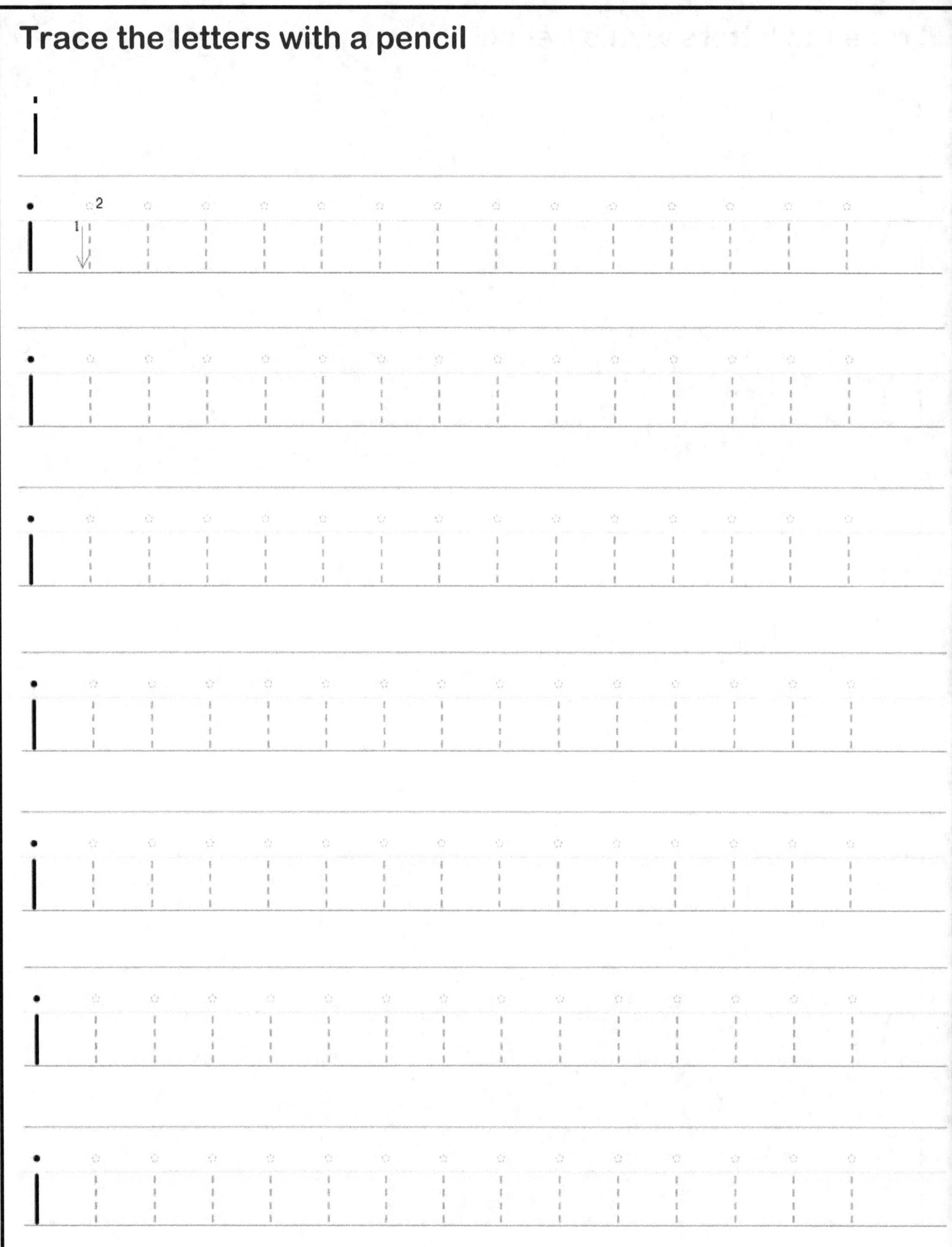

Trace the letters with a pencil

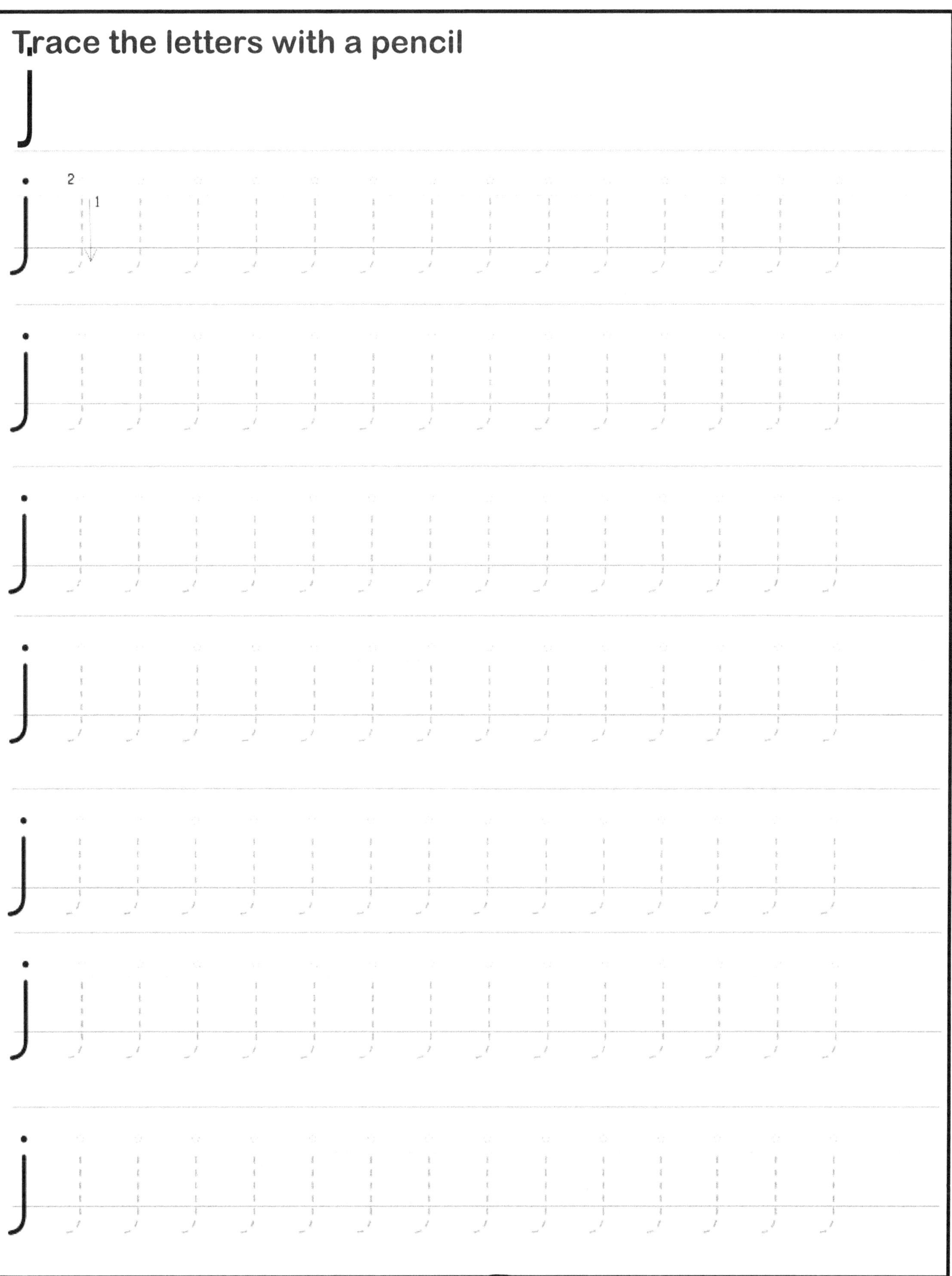

Trace the letters with a pencil

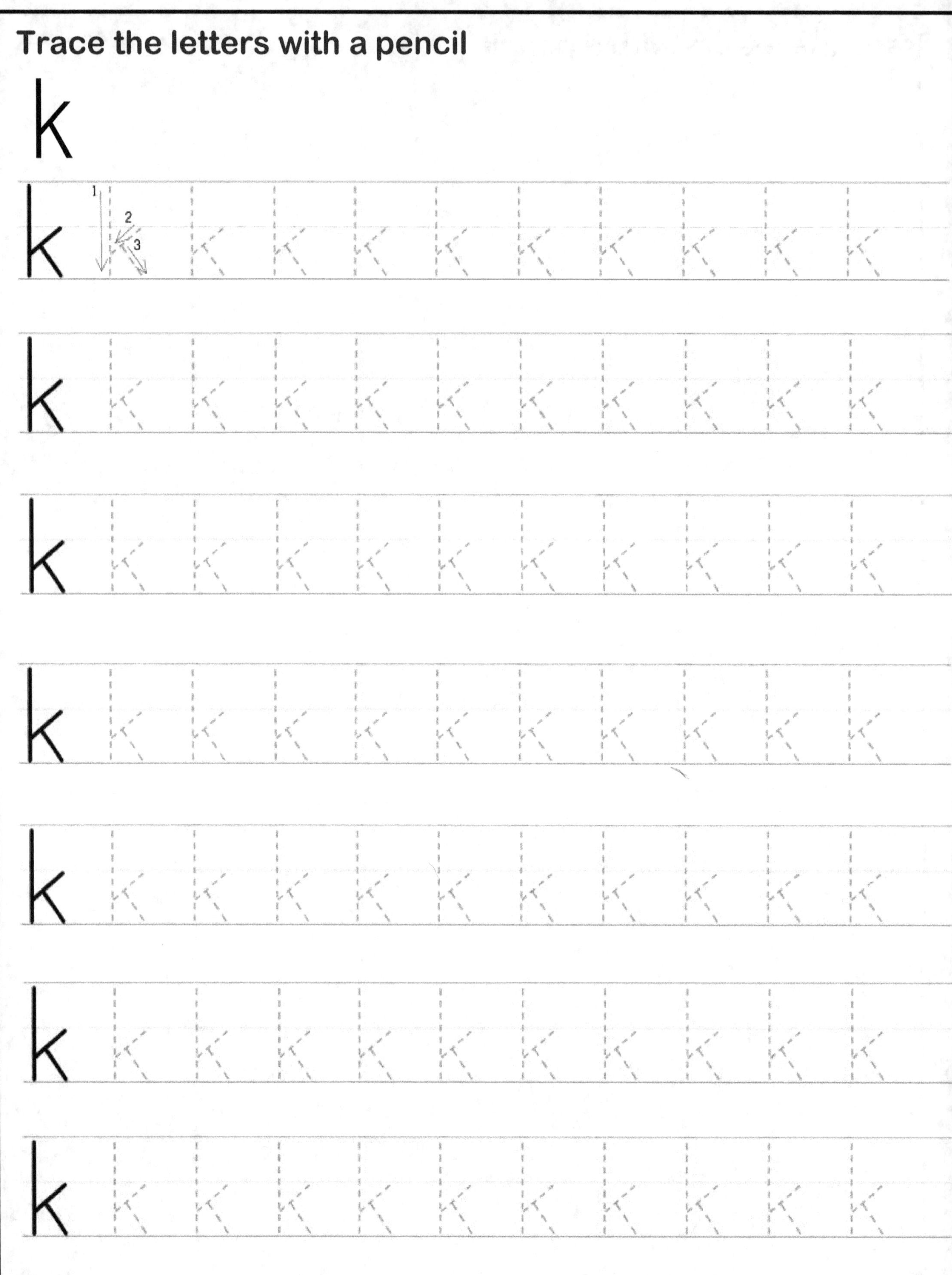

Trace the letters with a pencil

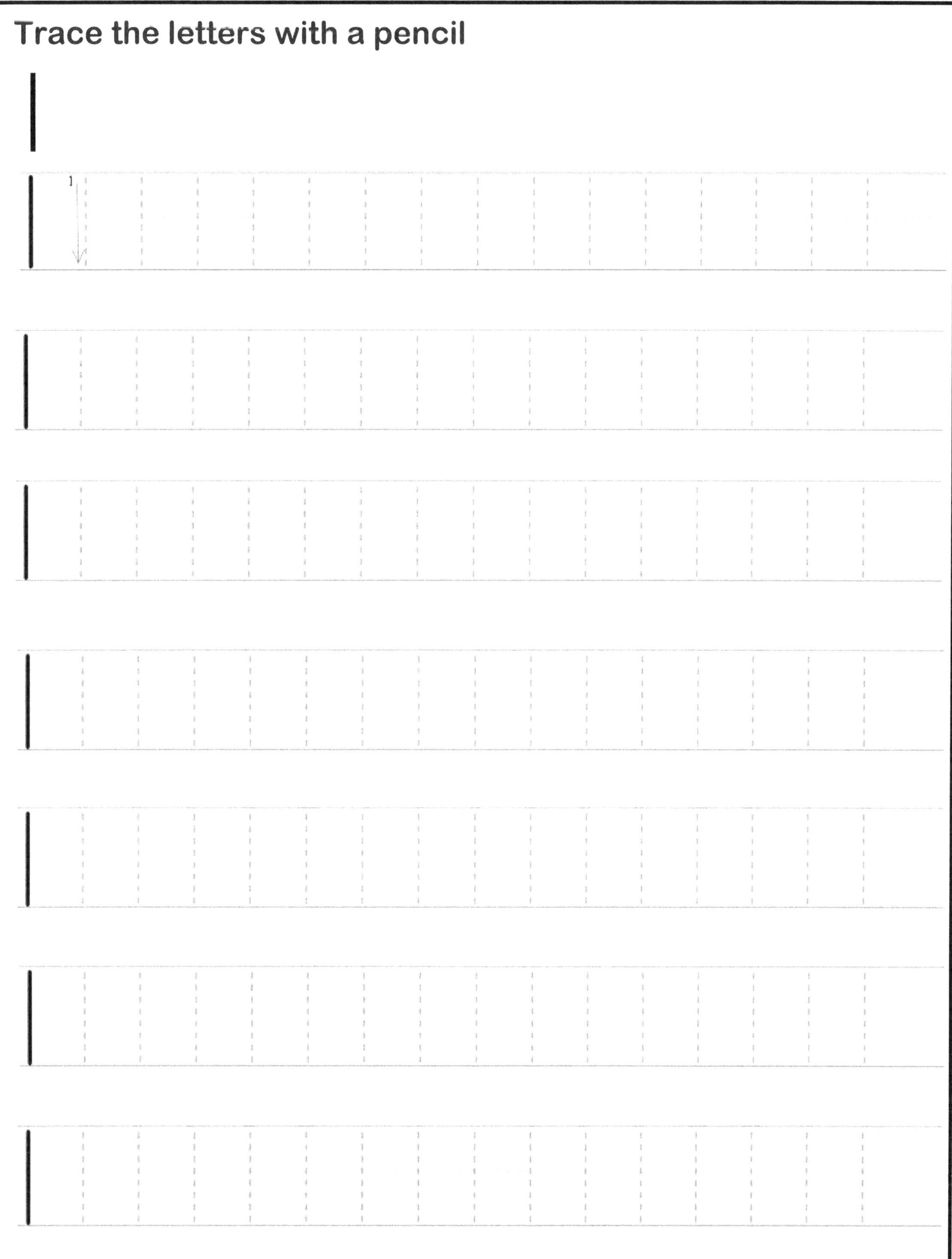

Trace the letters with a pencil

m

m 1 2 3 m m m m m m

m m m m m m m

m m m m m m m

m m m m m m m

m m m m m m m

m m m m m m m

m m m m m m m

Trace the letters with a pencil

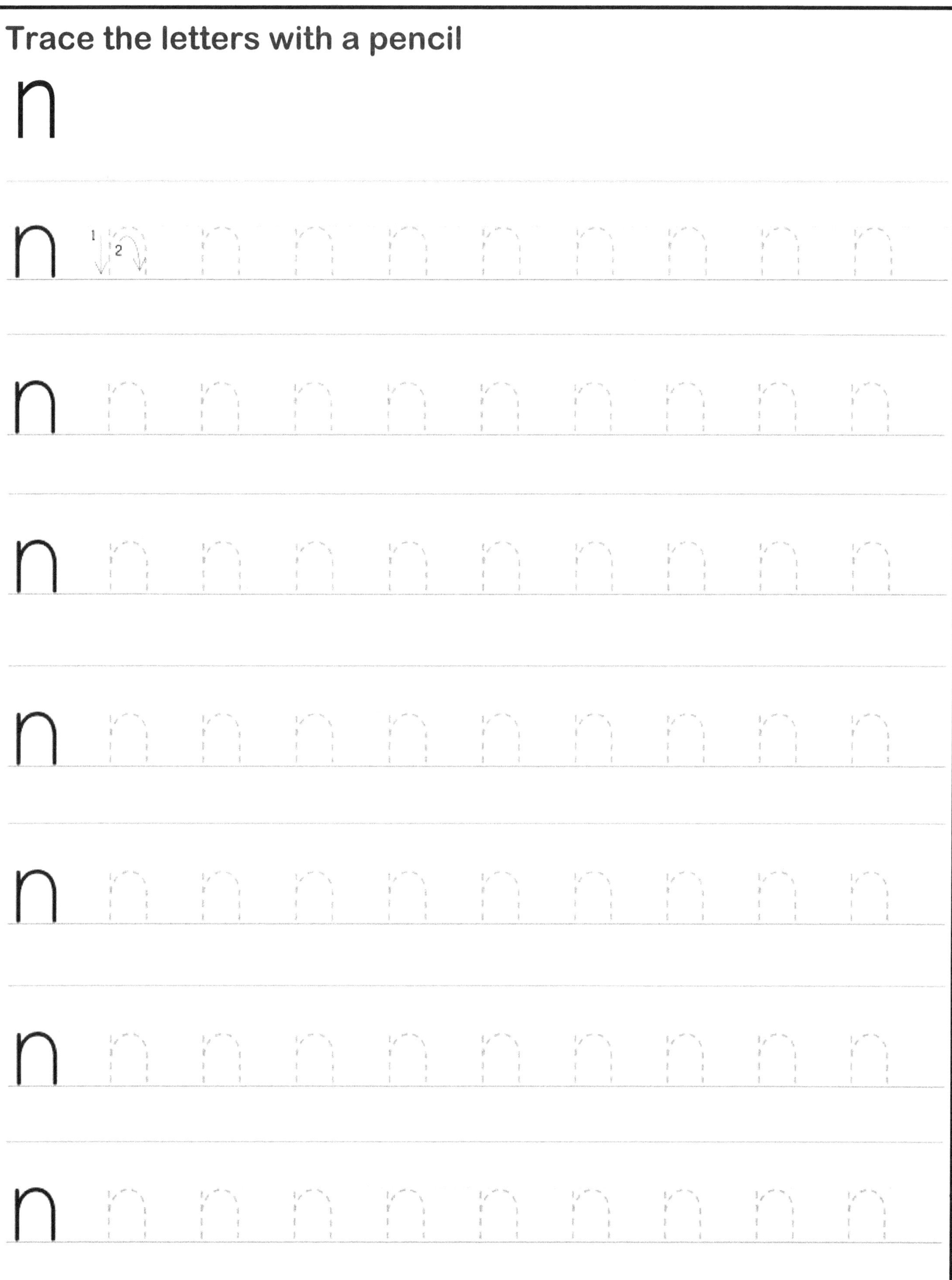

Trace the letters with a pencil

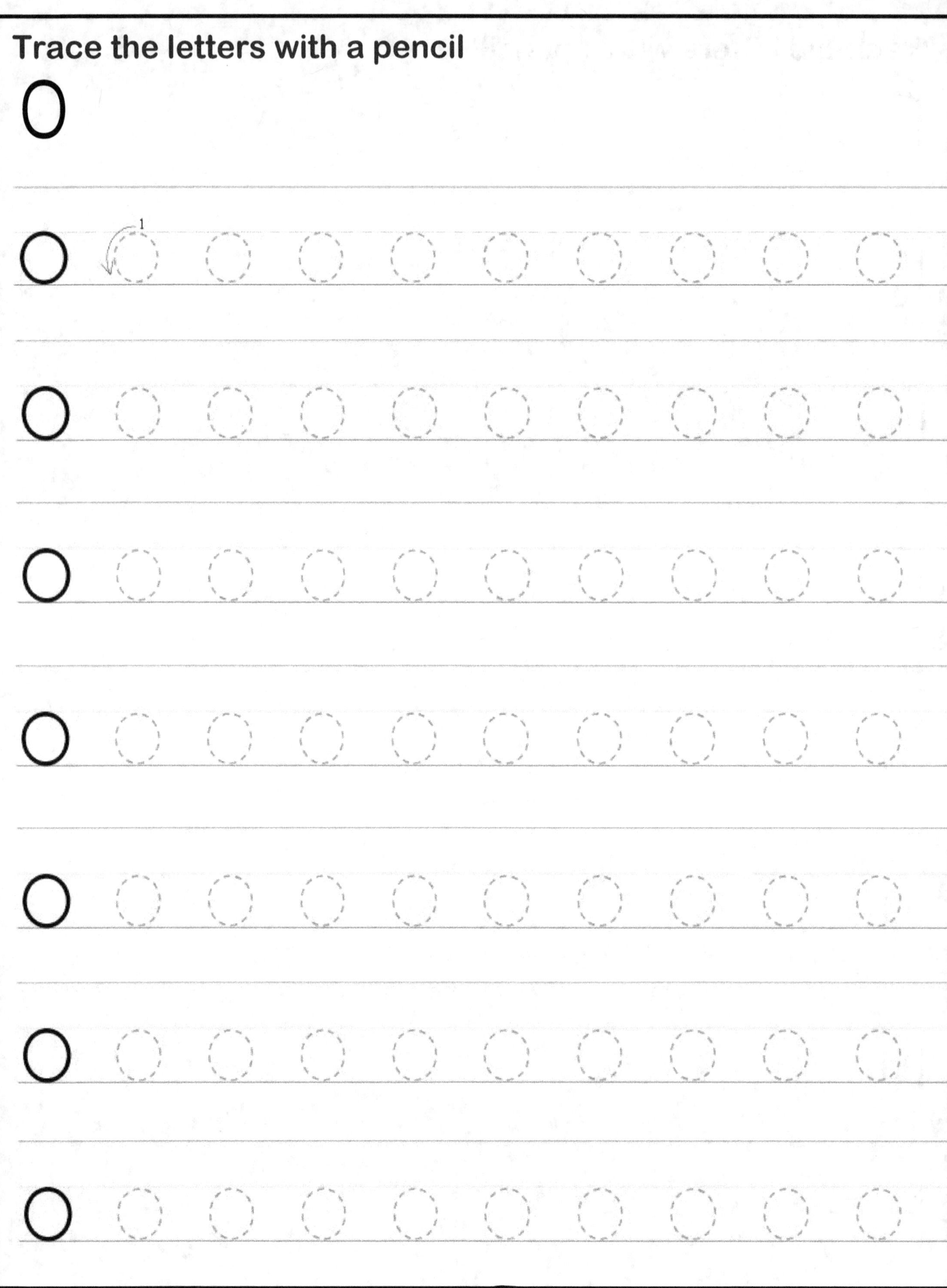

Trace the letters with a pencil

Trace the letters with a pencil

q

q 1 2

q

q

q

q

q

q

Trace the letters with a pencil

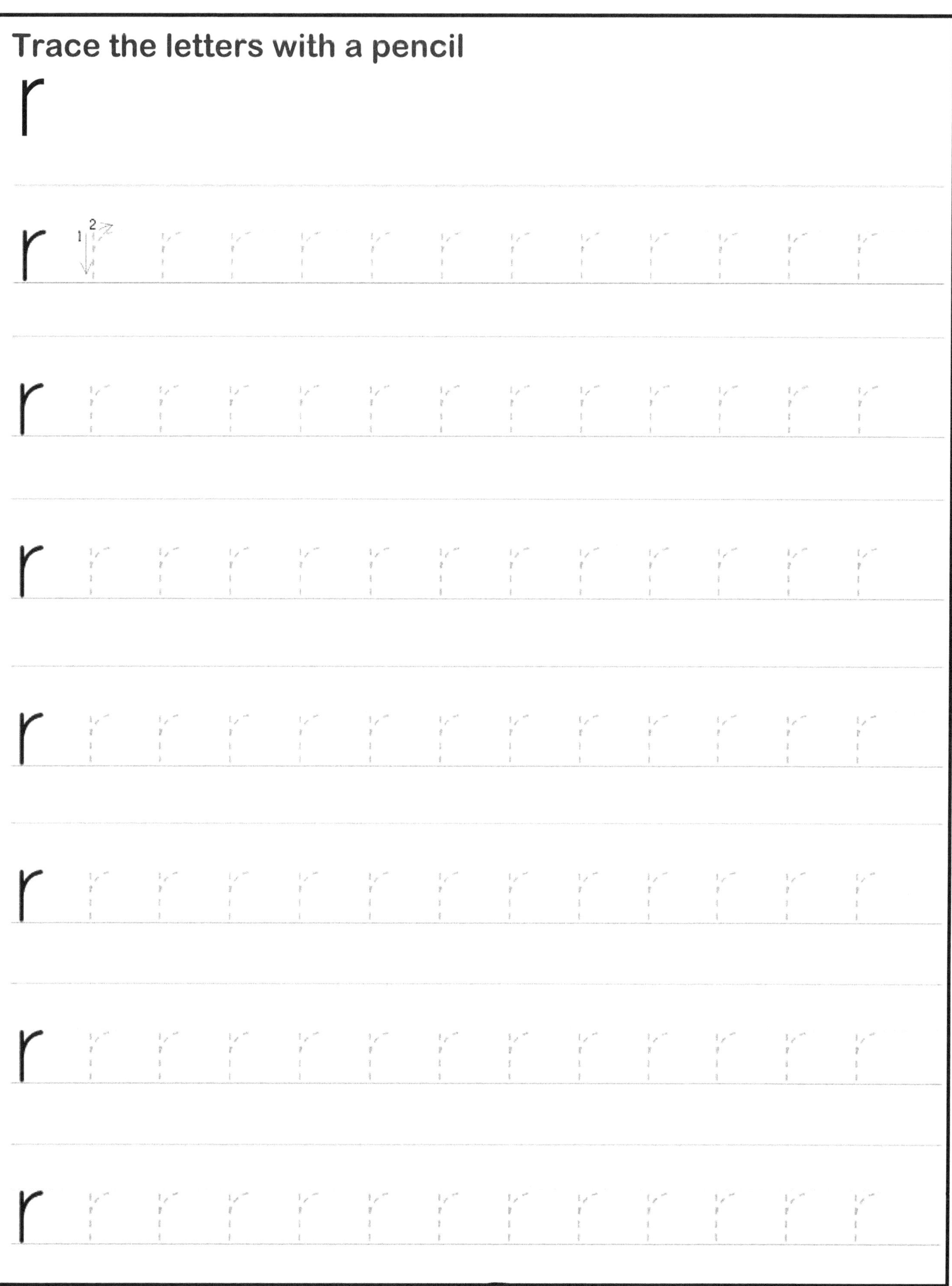

Trace the letters with a pencil

S

S S S S S S S S S S S

S S S S S S S S S S S

S S S S S S S S S S S

S S S S S S S S S S S

S S S S S S S S S S S

S S S S S S S S S S S

S S S S S S S S S S S

Trace the letters with a pencil

Trace the letters with a pencil

Trace the letters with a pencil

Trace the letters with a pencil

Trace the letters with a pencil

X

X 1 2

X

X

X

X

X

X

Trace the letters with a pencil

Trace the letters with a pencil

Z

Z 1 2 3

Z

Z

Z

Z

Z

Z

Trace and write the letters with a pencil below

A

A A A A A A A A A

1 2 3

a

a a a a a a a a a

1 2

Trace and write the letters with a pencil below

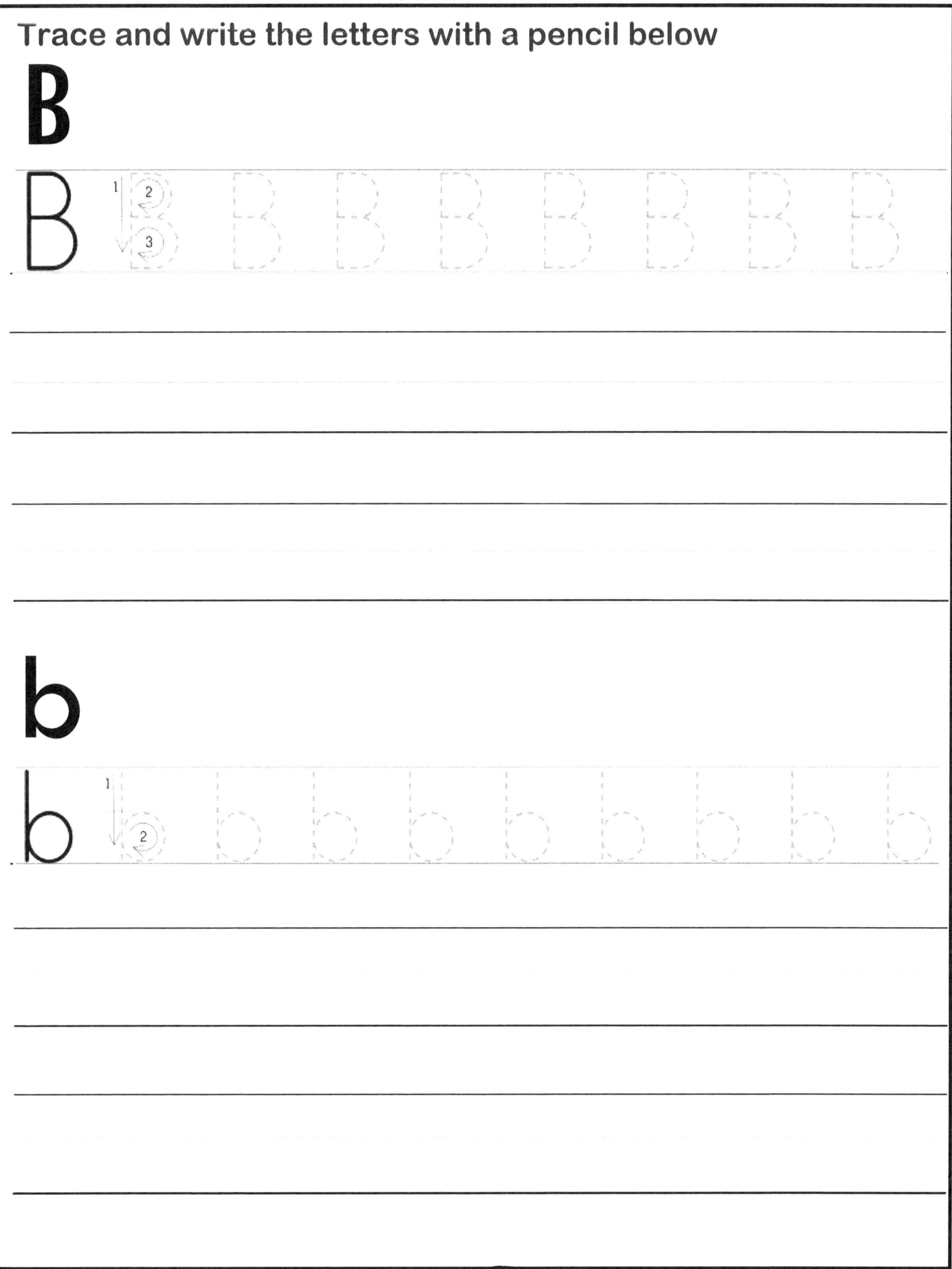

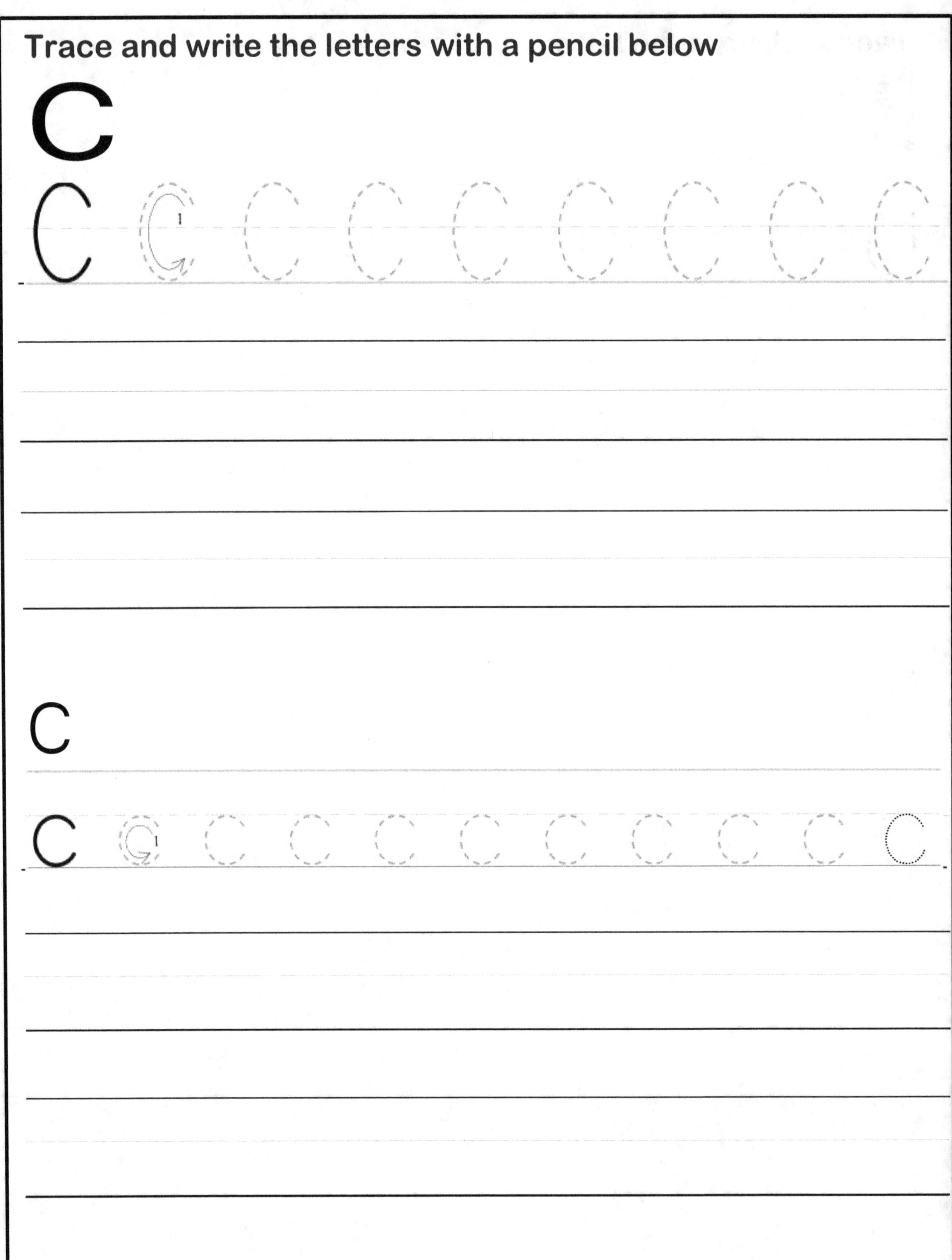
Trace and write the letters with a pencil below
C
C
c
c

Trace and write the letters with a pencil below

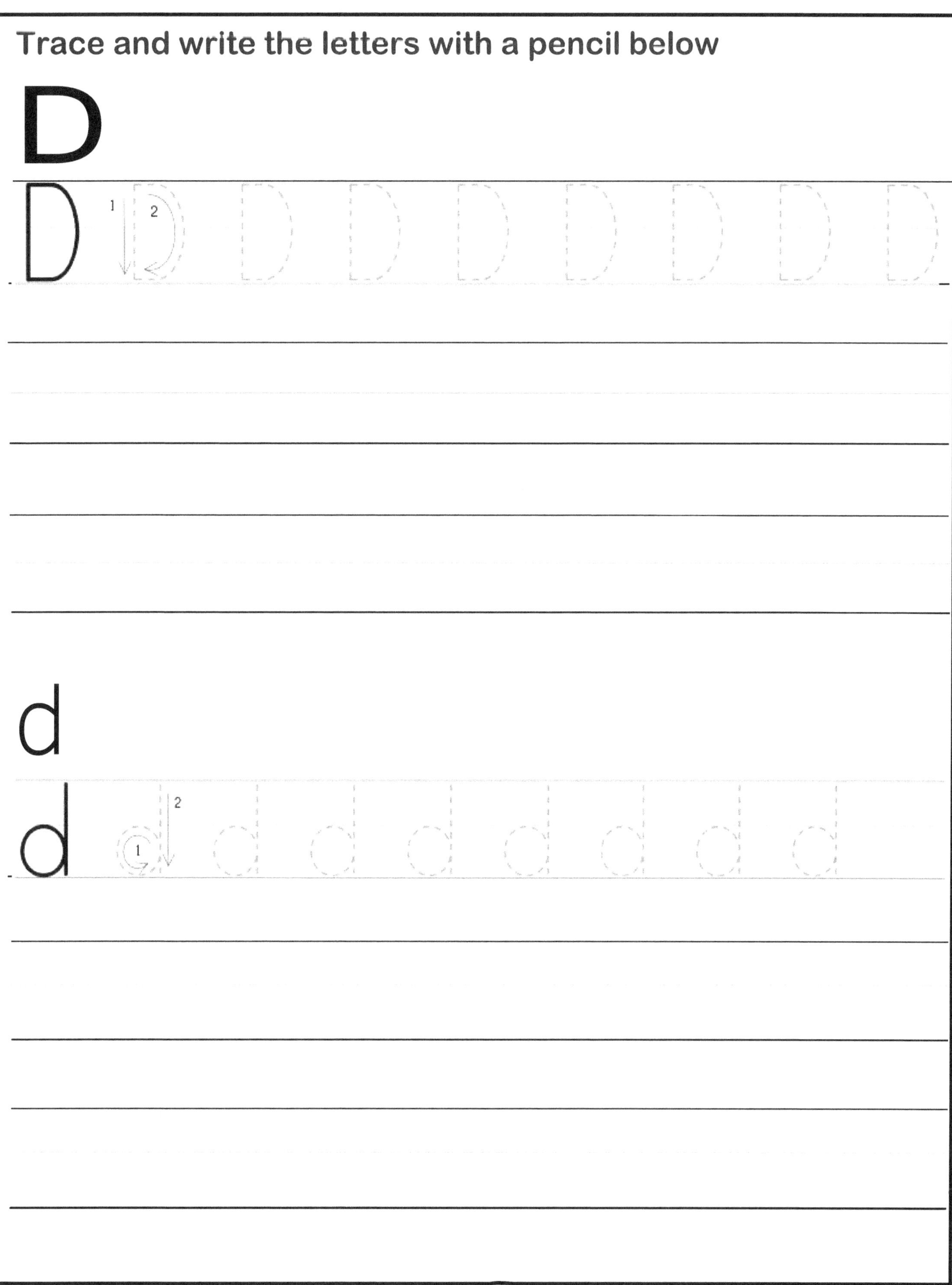

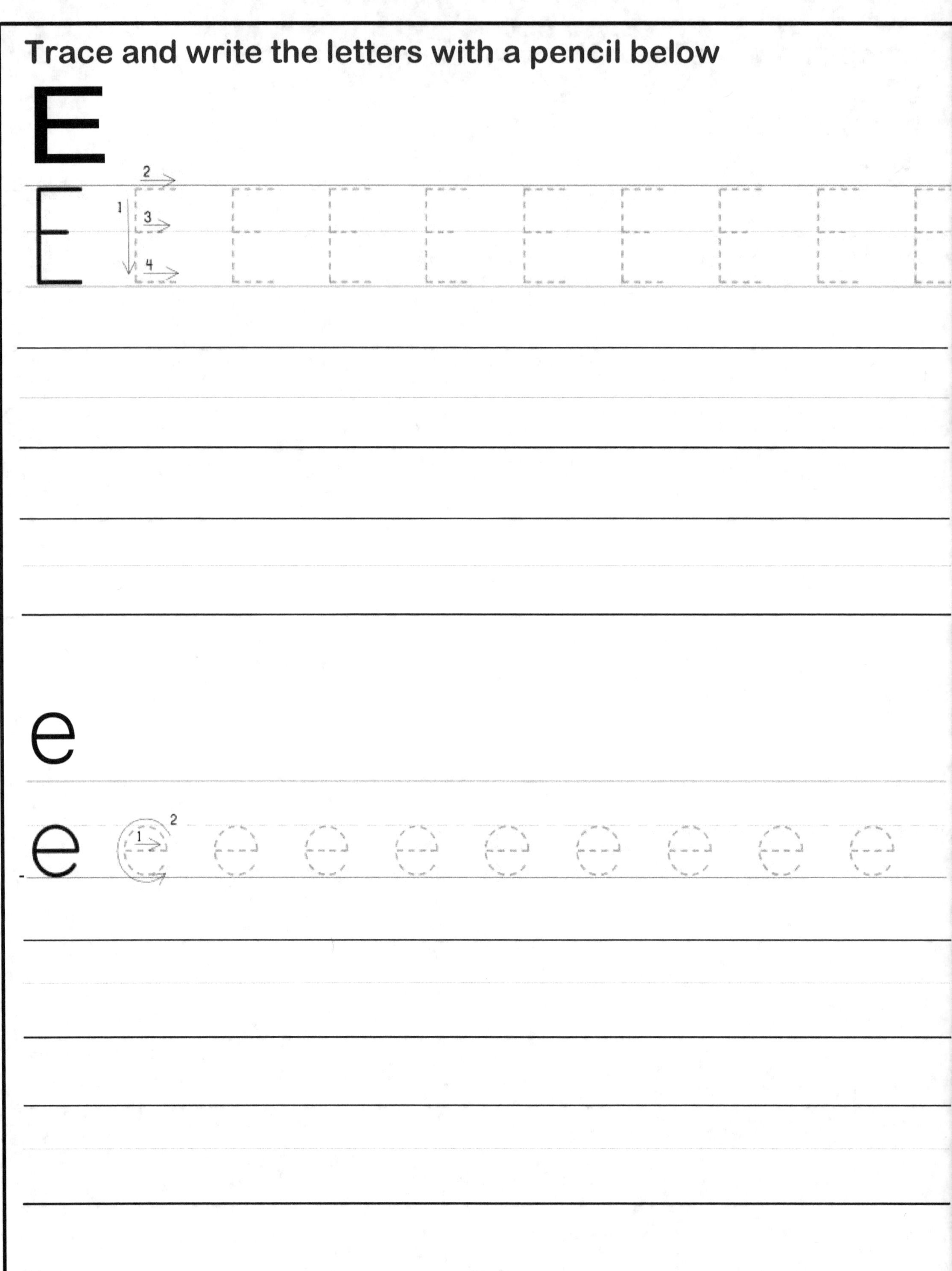
Trace and write the letters with a pencil below
E
E
1
2
3
4
e
e
1
2

Trace and write the letters with a pencil below

Trace and write the letters with a pencil below

G

G

g

g

Trace and write the letters with a pencil below

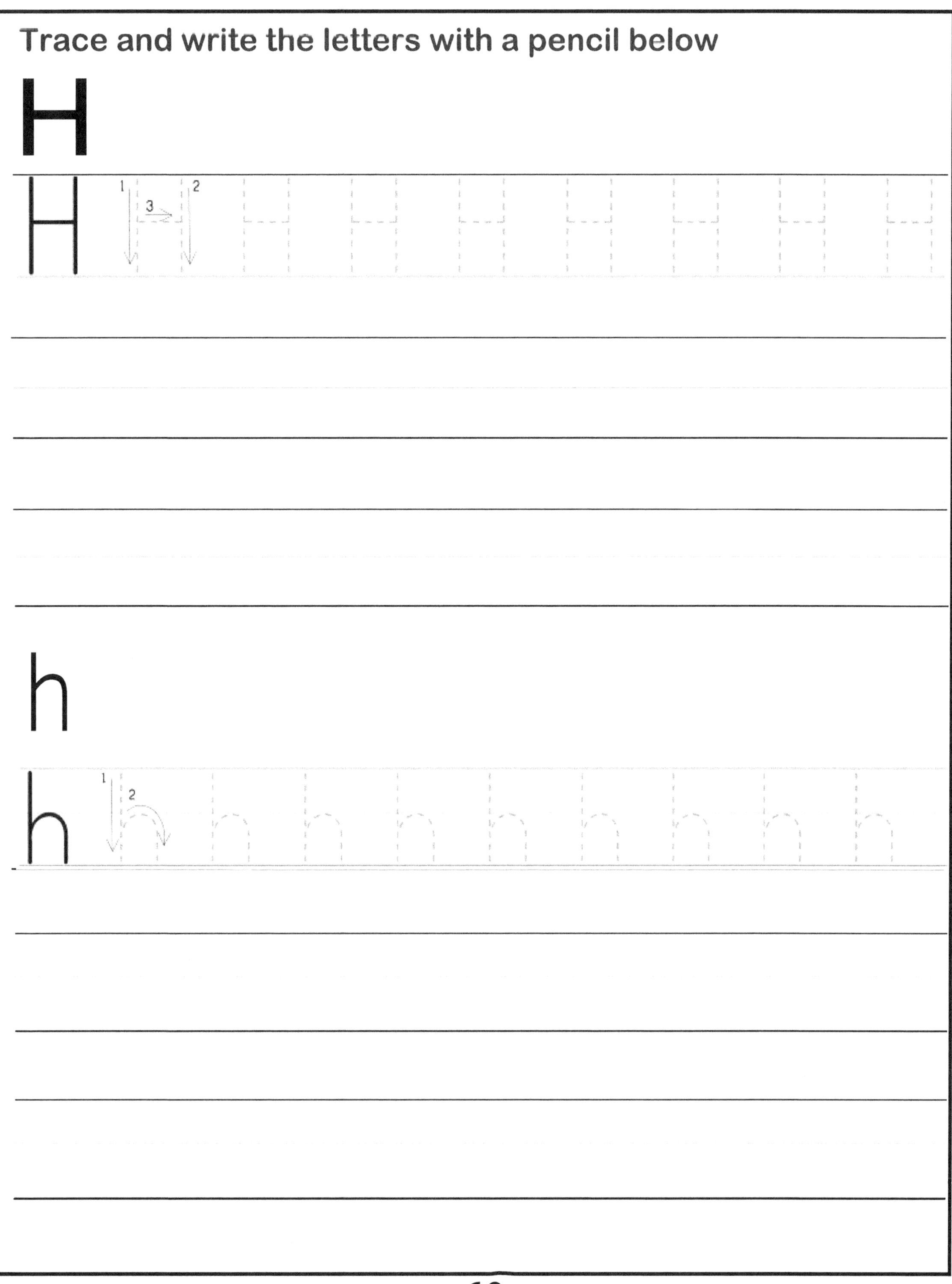

Trace and write the letters with a pencil below

Trace and write the letters with a pencil below

Trace and write the letters with a pencil below

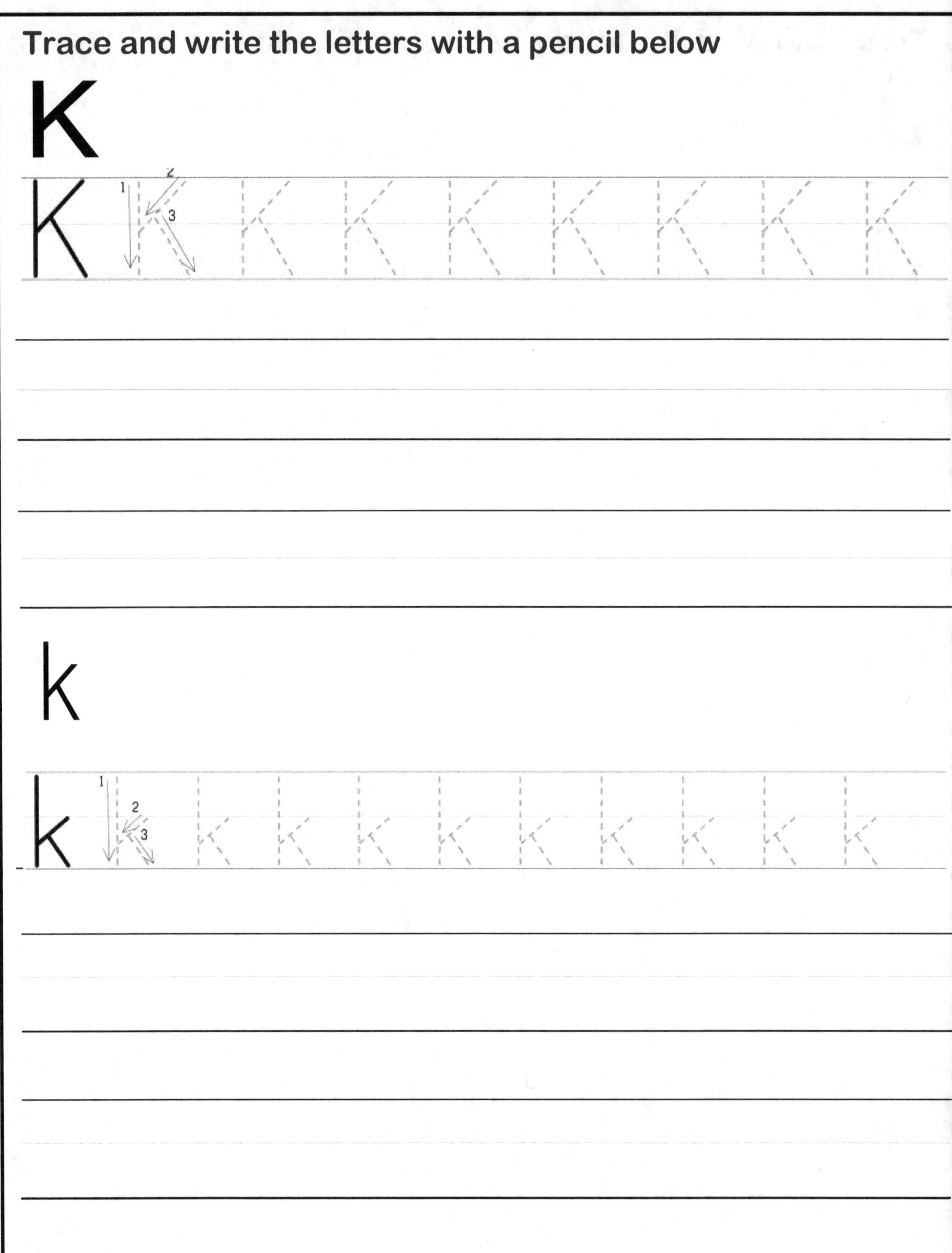

Trace and write the letters with a pencil below

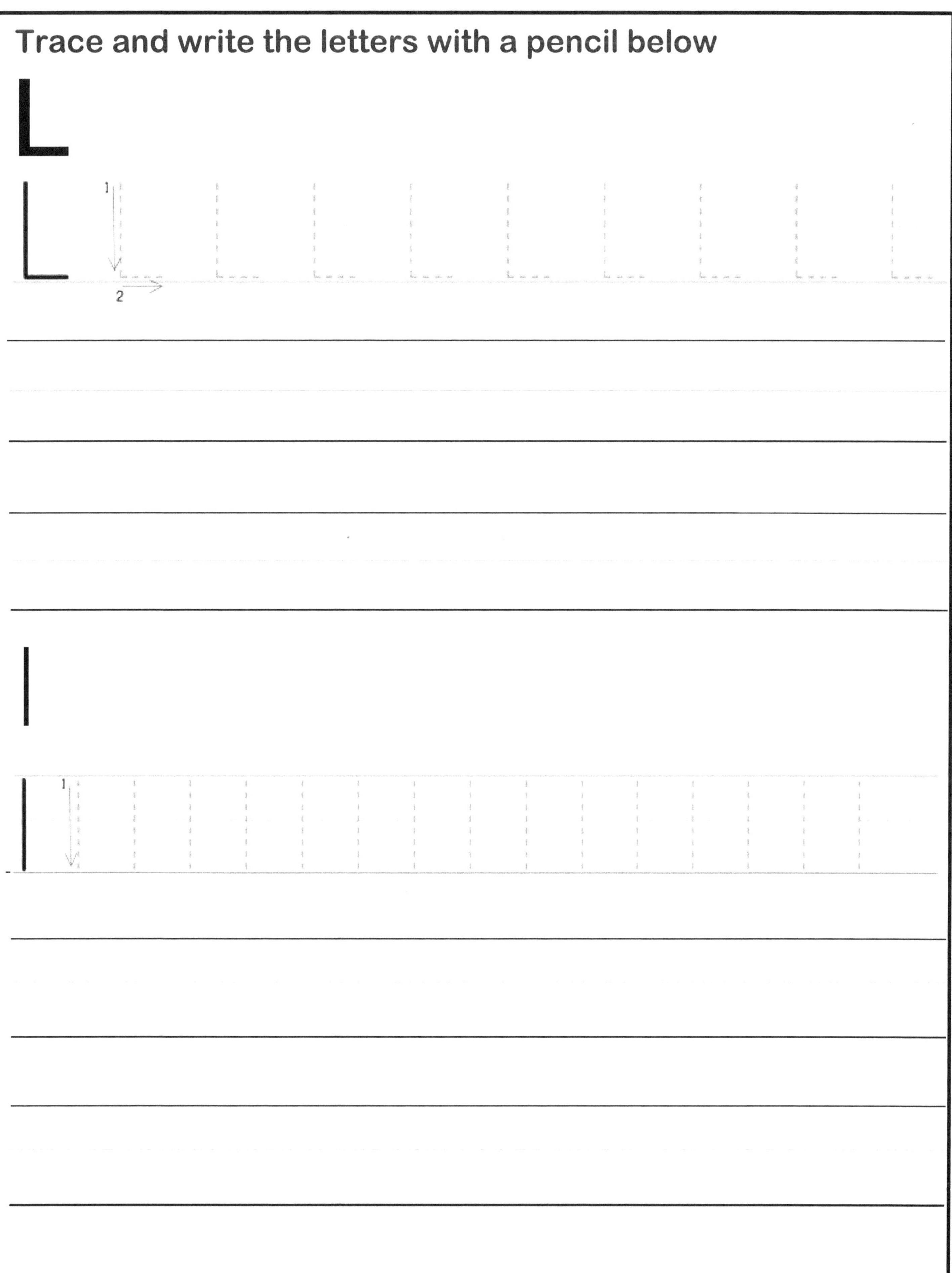

Trace and write the letters with a pencil below

M

M

m

m

Trace and write the letters with a pencil below

Trace and write the letters with a pencil below

Trace and write the letters with a pencil below

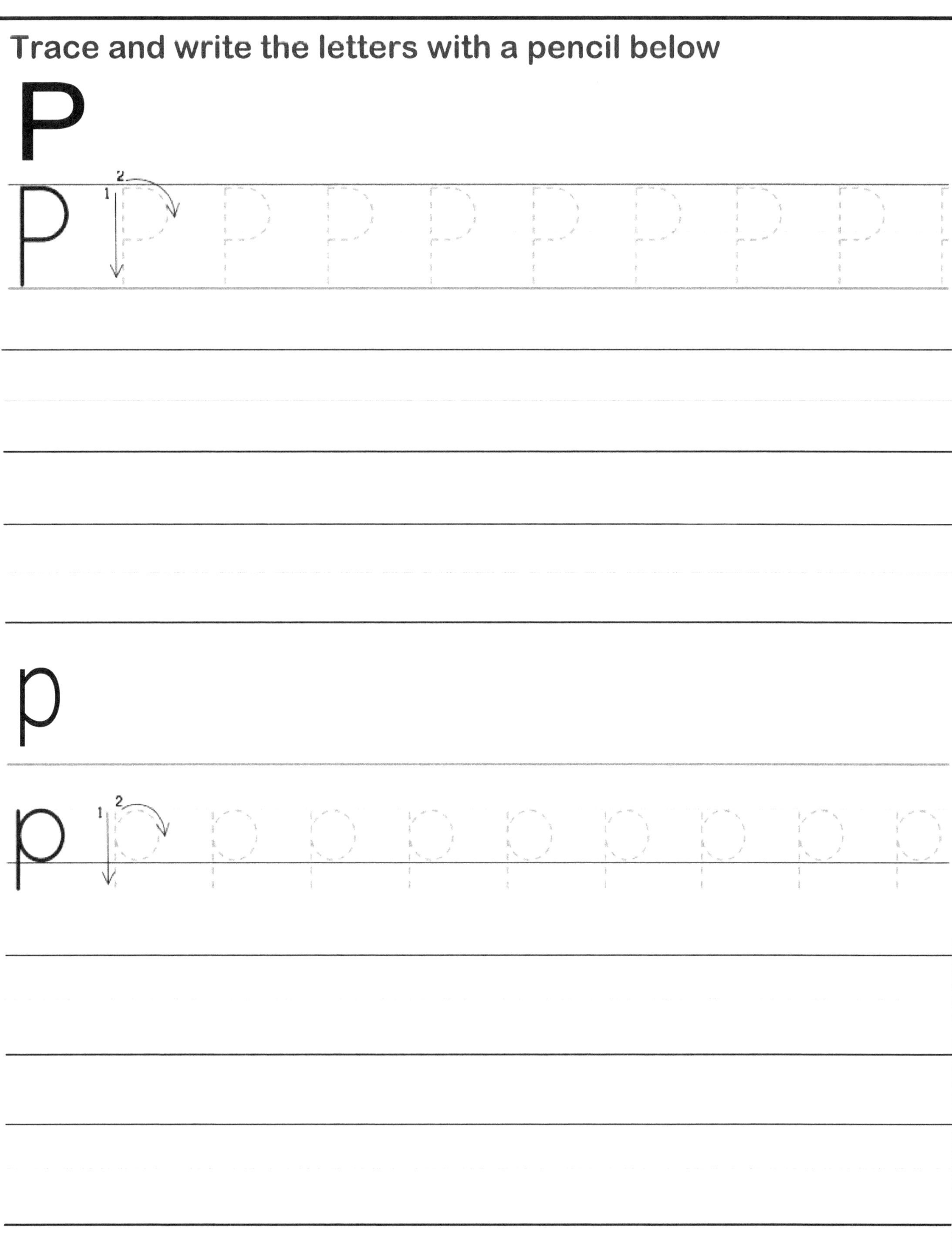

Trace and write the letters with a pencil below

Q

Q

q

q

Trace and write the letters with a pencil below
R
R
r
r

Trace and write the letters with a pencil below

Trace and write the letters with a pencil below

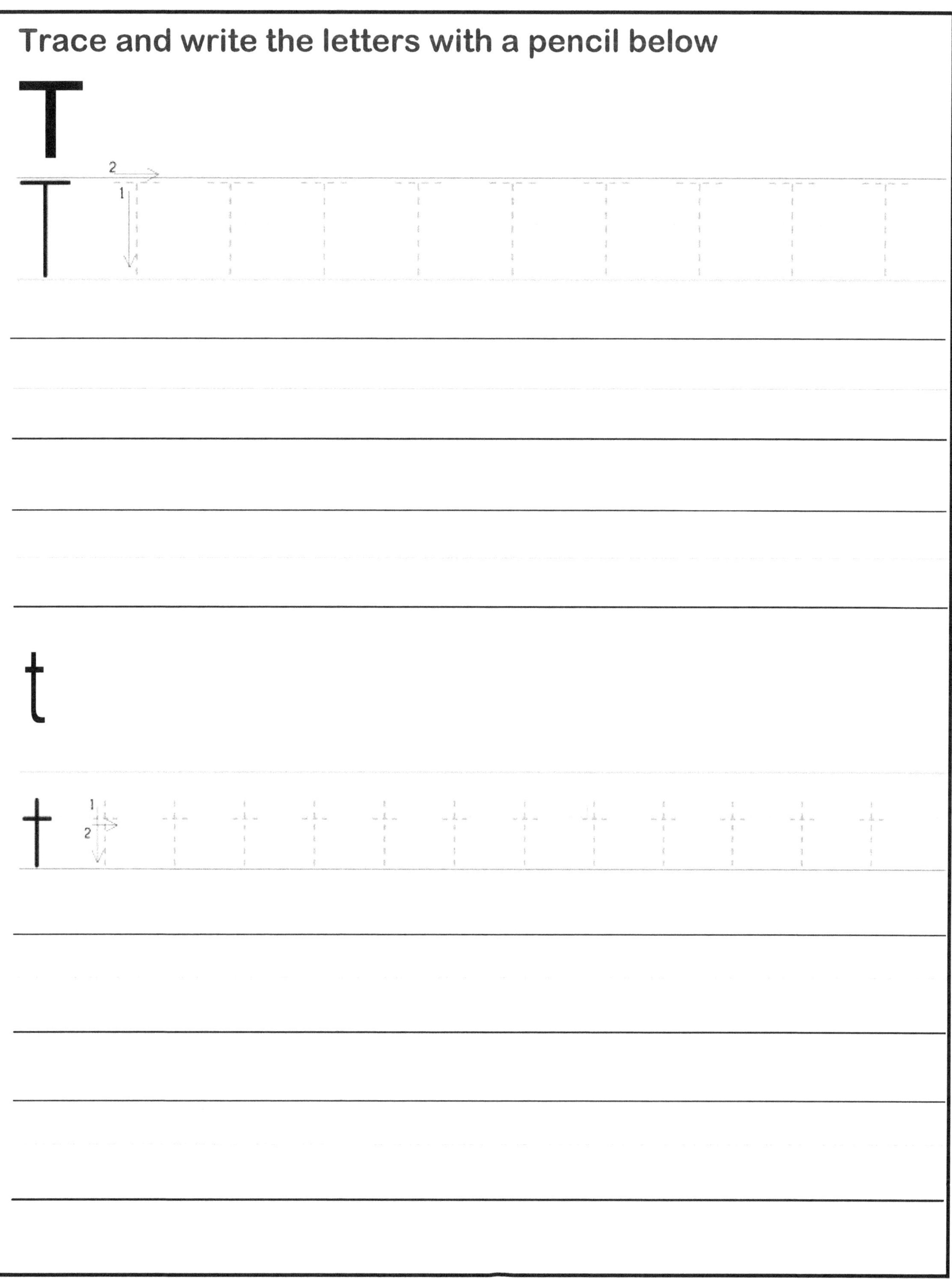

Trace and write the letters with a pencil below
U
U
1
u
u
1
2

Trace and write the letters with a pencil below

V

V 1 2

v

v 1 2

Trace and write the letters with a pencil below

W

W 1 2 3 4 W W W W W

w

w 1 2 3 4 w w w w w w w

Trace and write the letters with a pencil below

X

X 1 2

x

x 1 2

Trace and write the letters with a pencil below

Y

Y 1 2 3

y

y 1 2

Trace and write the letters with a pencil below

Z

Z

1 2 3

z

z

1 2 3

THE END

www.ingramcontent.com/pod-product-compliance
Lightning Source LLC
Chambersburg PA
CBHW060518120726
48002CB00011B/3217

* 9 7 9 8 6 4 2 4 8 2 3 4 6 *